RICHARD NERURKAR

MARATHON RUNNING

FROM BEGINNER TO ELITE

FOURTH EDITION

BLOOMSBURY

LONDON · NEW DELHI · NEW YORK · SYDNEY

For Bruce and Sue

Note

It is always the responsibility of the individual to assess his or her own fitness capability before participating in any training activity. While every effort has been made to ensure that the content of this book is as technically accurate and as sound as possible, neither the author nor the publishers can accept responsibility for any injury or loss sustained as a result of the use of this material.

Published by Bloomsbury Publishing Plc
50 Bedford Square
London WC1B 3DP
www.bloomsbury.com

Fourth edition 2012
Third edition 2008
Second edition 2004
First edition 2000

Copyright © 2012, 2008, 2004, 2000 Richard Ner

ISBN (print) 978 1 4081 6066 4
ISBN (EPUB) 978 1 4081 7868 3
ISBN (EPDF) 978 1 4081 7867 6

Richard Nerurkar has asserted his rights under the Copyright, Design and Patents Act, 1988, to be identified as the author of this work.

A CIP catalogue record for this book is available from the British Library.

Acknowledgements
Cover photograph © Shutterstock
Inside photographs pp. vi, xi, xiii, xv, 4, 28, 39, 47, 51, 65, 84, 91, 92 x 2, 109, 110 x 2, 118, 123, 124, 129, 132, 135, 138, 145, 148, 150, 152, 154, 161, 170, 173, 178 x 2, 183, 186, 191, 192, 200, 216 and 217 © Mark Shearman; pp. ix, xvi © Ashenafi Gudeta; pp. 6, 7, 8 and 9 © Grant Pritchard; p. 16 © James MacDonald; pp. 2, 19, 48, 61 x 2, 74, 102, 131, 157, 162, 165, 169 x 2, 172, 196 and 197 © Jiro Mochizuki; pp. 87, 105, 140, 174 © JJ Waller; p. 81 © Skye Blackpool; pp. 18, 41, 116, 143, 184, and 189 author's own

Designed by James Watson
Commissioned by Charlotte Croft
Edited by Sarah Cole

This book is produced using paper that is made from wood grown in managed, sustainable forests. It is natural, renewable and recyclable. The logging and manufacturing processes conform to the environmental regulations of the country of origin.

Typeset in URW Grotesk by seagulls.net

Printed and bound in India by Replika Press Pvt Ltd

10 9 8 7 6 5 4 3 2 1

CONTENTS

FOREWORD

As a sporting event the marathon is unique in many ways. In no other event could absolute beginners find themselves lining up alongside world champions and record holders with a common goal at a shared time and place. No matter what your standard, to conquer the 26.2-mile distance requires immense determination and a huge physical effort.

Richard Nerurkar had the supreme ability of making the whole thing look a lot less daunting. As Britain's most successful marathon runner during the 90s, he applied thought and practicality to his training, which took him among the world's elite. Winning the World Cup in San Sebastian in 1993 gave him the impetus to shoot for the World and Olympic titles. If all this book did was tell the story of Richard's personal challenges to reach the very top then that would be enthralling enough. But he has cleverly used his career landmarks to outline the building blocks for a successful marathon, whether you are a first-timer or a seasoned campaigner. He intertwines his own marathon experiences with clear and practical information and advice on how to plan your training, diet, race tactics, recuperation and much more. Each chapter has the key points summarised, making the book very easy to use.

Richard was a tough competitor and a meticulous planner. Here, he has taken some of the hard work out of running the marathon for those who aim to follow in his steps. It will never be easy, as I now know, but this book should act as a guide for all marathoners – even for those of us who think we know a thing or two about running.

Steve Cram

The start of the men's marathon at the 2011 World Championships in Daegu

NOTES ON TERMINOLOGY

TABLE 0.1 KILOMETRES TO MILES – CONVERSION

km	miles
1	0.6
5	3.1
10	6.2
15	9.4
20	12.5
21	13.1
25	15.6
30	18.8
42	26.2

TABLE 0.2 TRAINING TYPE DEFINITIONS

Repetitions ('reps')	Efforts of fast running over a short distance, followed by a period of recovery – the cycle being repeated a number of times
Fartlek	Literally 'speed-play'. A combination of fast and slow running, often based on a more flexible pattern of time/distance and effort/recovery
Tempo run	A single effort of sustained fast running
Pyramid	A session alternating easy jogging with brisk running – usually building up to a peak of either duration or intensity, and then declining again
Strides	Fast, but not flat-out sprinting over a short distance

CATEGORIES OF RUNNER

- **Beginner:** Starting running 'from scratch'
- **First time marathon runner:** Perhaps a regular runner, but a newcomer to the marathon
- **Advanced:** aiming to complete a marathon in under 3 hours
- **Elite:** Aiming to complete a marathon in under 2.5 hours.

RUNNING DISTANCES – MILES VERSUS KILOMETRES

Whereas in other European countries runners refer to distances in kilometres rather than miles, the reverse is more often the case in Britain. Yet even in Britain, certain set distances in kilometres – such as road races over 10km – are familiar concepts to many runners.

Working in kilometres has a dual advantage: first, kilometres pass more quickly than miles and thus give you more reference points over the course of a long run; and second, in your training they allow you to mimic the system used at most major marathons, where drink stations are placed every 5km along the route. Strength of tradition and habit will probably ensure, however, that you end up working in miles.

For the purposes of this book, accepted 'running parlance' has been used. Reference can be made, as useful or necessary, to the conversions in Table 0.1 (equating to the common reference points during the course of a marathon).

PREFACE TO THE FOURTH EDITION

Some years ago I was invited to a new running event in Mumbai, which happened to be India's first serious attempt at mass-participation running. Twenty-four hours before the race I found myself sitting alongside the one-lap world record holder Michael Johnson and fielding questions seminar-style about how best to run a marathon. The double Olympic champion was handed the microphone first. 'Don't ask me,' came the answer in his Texan drawl, 'I'm a sprinter, not a runner.'

Using Johnson's terminology, sprinting and specifically the athlete Usain Bolt have gone a long way in winning back the public's interest in athletics in recent years. Meanwhile, the running boom continues unabated at a mass level. In Britain several new marathon races have emerged in Brighton, Chester and Milton Keynes (to name just a few). Liverpool and Manchester have their own city marathons and at the global level, the series of races known as the World Marathon Majors comprising the big-city marathons of London, Boston, Berlin, Chicago and New York, surpass record participation numbers with each passing year.

Two other developments reinforce this upward trend in marathon running. The first is the continued success of the marathon as a vehicle for raising money for charity. The annual London Marathon, now in its 31st year, has become the biggest single fundraising event in Britain with more than £50 million raised for charities annually.

The other big issue back in the spotlight in world marathon running is the speculation on when the first sub-two hour marathon might be achieved. When the third edition of this book came out in 2008, Ethiopia's Haile Gebrselassie had just improved his own world record by 27 seconds when he became the first runner to run the marathon in under 2 hours and 4 minutes (2:03:59). This record is now currently held by the Kenyan Patrick Makau who ran 2:03:38 on the same Berlin course in September 2011, although judging by the amazing depth of world-class marathoners emerging from Kenya (Makau's compatriot Wilson Kipsang ran 2:03:42 in Frankfurt one month after the Berlin race), it appears that this mark has an insecure future. Today, winning times of 2:04 and 2:05 from both Kenyan and Ethiopian athletes have become commonplace in many big-city marathons – a far cry from 19 years ago when Britain's Eamonn Martin won the London Marathon in a time of 2:10:50 and I achieved victory in my debut marathon in Hamburg in 2:10:57 (see p. 23). In this new edition, I join this debate by reflecting on what it will take to achieve a sub-two hour time at the marathon (see p. 130).

Inevitably, the names and faces of the athletes grabbing the marathon headlines have moved on from when I wrote this book's first edition in 2000. The likes of Thugwane, Tergat, Baldini and Khannouchi have retired; the superlative career of Britain's greatest female marathon runner Paula Radcliffe (featured on the front cover of the book's second edition) is drawing to a close, and, although he has proved me wrong before (for example, by resurrecting his international track career in Beijing four years ago), the amazing career of Haile Gebrselassie is now surely in its twilight period. This edition includes a number of updated images of both Haile and Paula, friends whom I admire not least for their 'never-say-die' approach to their sport.

Going back to that question in Mumbai, the answer I gave then has changed little over the years: there are still no shortcuts to the thrill of finishing a marathon. But as everyone continues to tell me – as you'll read in some of the additional personal experiences recounted in this new edition – the marathon challenge is still worth it in the end and your memories of it will stay with you for life.

Richard Nerurkar
Brighton
January 2012

Paula Radcliffe alongside Derartu Tulu, Tirunesh Dibaba and Haile Gebrselassie on her visit to Addis Ababa in November 2009

INTRODUCTION
TAKING UP THE CHALLENGE OF THE MARATHON

'You must be crazy – just thinking of it makes me tired.'

**'I don't know how you do it – I can't even run
to the end of the street!'**

'What do you think of for all that time?'

'Don't you get a lot of injuries?'

'Do you do it for a living?'

'Are you allowed to eat chocolate?'

These are just some people's reactions when I introduce myself as 'a marathon runner'. For some, the thought of running a marathon is not far short of their worst nightmare. For others, the reaction is rather one of amazement as they try to imagine what it must be like to cover – on foot and at speed – such a long distance. Still others are curious about how it is achieved. Some are filled with admiration; few are moved by envy; many simply want to encourage me on towards my goal.

Love it or hate it, people are fascinated by the marathon. When I tell them what I do, whether they react with curiosity or amazement, I know straight away that even without having run a marathon they have a sense of what's involved. People recognise that running a marathon involves a lot of effort and hard work. I may have a certain amount of talent to run well, but talent on its own doesn't count for very much unless I go out and do the training. That's true about anyone, at any level, wishing to run a marathon.

To rise to the challenge of the marathon and complete the 26-mile distance involves a huge expenditure of effort and determination.

There is also a certain mystique about the event. Although you may have some idea of what's involved, until you've run your first marathon it's hard to appreciate the true nature of the marathon experience. It's one thing to observe the expressions of joy and relief of weary runners staggering exhausted over the finishing line, but it's quite another matter suffering those extremes of fatigue yourself as you fight your way to the end of the race. You might have a sense of how cruel the event can be from having seen runners collapse on the roadside, but without actually putting yourself through the same degree of exhaustion, how can you know what this feels like – or how in similar situations, other runners survive and drag themselves to the finish? Watching a marathon on television is worlds apart from experiencing it first-hand.

So what motivates people to run marathons? Let's face it, running is a simple activity. From early childhood it is one of our most natural activities. It requires effort, but not much technical expertise. As we leave our childhood behind, many of us grow out of the habit – which is why the thought of running even to the end of the street seems like hard work. The good news is, however, that with a little bit of training – or retraining – we can rediscover the ability to run. Of course, running in our adulthood involves more effort than it did when we were children, but once you have set yourself the goal of getting fit, the habit can be quickly relearned. For many, the next step up from wanting to get fit is deciding to run a marathon. It sounds crazy, I know, but it also speaks volumes for the special appeal of the 26-mile distance.

For running novices, the marathon offers a great challenge – accessible to and understood by many, but only

Marathon runners often dress for the occasion in the weird and wonderful

accomplished by those brave enough to take the plunge. True, your training for the marathon will exhaust you and you might get to the finish of the race vowing never to run another one. But to have actually run a marathon represents a highly satisfying feat of willpower and endurance. Many runners decide to run a marathon having first watched countless others – slower, less athletic and more overweight than themselves – do precisely that in Britain's most famous and popular road race, the London Marathon.

Today, many people who are drawn into running marathons are also motivated by the desire to help other people by raising money and awareness for charity. 'If I'm going to put myself through the pain of running a marathon,' so their reasoning goes, 'at least I want to do it for a good cause.' Besides, why else would runners get dressed up as waiters, rhinos, toucans and superducks – and then attempt to run 26 miles?!

> **'You may be in the same race as three or 30,000 others, but essentially the contest is between you and the distance.'**

For regular runners, there may be a sense of not having completed one's running experience without having run a marathon. They feel they owe it to themselves to run one, not necessarily to achieve a certain time or position in a certain race, but rather to experience for themselves what the marathon is really like. The marathon is also a good yardstick by which they can assess (and profess) their running ability: to say that you are 'a 3½-hour marathon runner' sounds much more impressive than to profess to being 'a 75-minute 10-mile runner'. For many other regular runners, the marathon represents their one major goal for the year, and the result by which they compare their running fortunes from one year to the next.

For elite athletes, the marathon may appeal for no better reason than that they are good at it. For sure, they enjoy the feeling of fitness and the process of training. But beyond this, there is the satisfaction of being able to perform at a level considerably above the capabilities of the ordinary person. These considerations outweigh the fact that a lot of effort and hard work, not to mention pain, is involved in the process of producing good results.

So, what's special about the marathon? First, everyone's a winner. The challenge is to cover 26 miles and 385 yards. You may be in the same race as three or 30,000 others, but essentially the contest is between you and the distance. For most runners taking part in a big-city marathon, 'winning' means conquering the distance. It's also the only sporting competition where first-time marathon runners can 'toe the line' alongside Olympic champions. Even if you do not have a resting pulse of 32, weigh less than 60kg, and run 120 miles a week, marathon running need not remain a passive interest. Whatever your background, the challenge is open to anyone prepared to commit themselves to the task of covering the distance.

As well as wondering what is so special about the marathon, people frequently ask, 'What do you get out of it?' Although this will obviously differ from person to person, most marathon runners will probably agree on the following:

- *It gives your life a focus*. To decide to run a marathon is like embarking on a mission. First-time marathon runners attempt to achieve a goal previously considered unimaginable. Many enjoy the sense of purpose gained from following a structured training programme. Experienced runners use the marathon as a pretext for adopting a more serious approach to their training at the start of their marathon build-up. As your marathon draws near, it's hard not to let the thought of the race, let alone your training and preparation, impinge on other areas of your life.

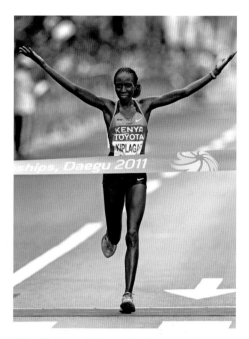

- *It's a shared experience.* Due to the growth in popularity of running over the past 30 years, the days of the lonely long-distance runner have become largely a thing of the past. Whatever standard of runner you are, training partners are at hand to accompany you on your weekend long run, or an evening session down at your local club. Even if you find yourself doing much of your running on your

Edna Kiplagat of Kenya wins the women's marathon at the 2011 World Championships in Daegu

own in the build-up to a marathon, the thought of other runners working towards the same goal might spur you on in your training. You might also find that your non-running friends start to become interested in your marathon ambitions and share some of your excitement.

- *It's a personal achievement.* Most people who watch the London Marathon, while perhaps admiring the few gaunt-looking athletes at the front of the race, are more likely to identify with the thousands behind them whose only goal may be simply to get to the finish. These runners are not universally successful in achieving their time goal for the distance, nor do they always raise quite as much money for charity as they might first have hoped. Nevertheless, simply getting to the finish of the marathon represents a huge personal achievement.

However, while it's easy to romanticise the marathon experience – rising to challenges; fulfilling long-held ambitions; the exhilaration of performing at your best; enjoying a deep sense of satisfaction – the bottom line is that it is *tough*. It requires a great deal of hard training, sacrifices in terms of both time and energy, and lots of grit and determination to overcome those feelings of tiredness and pain. If you are thinking about running a marathon, think hard and carefully. It's a big commitment, yet if you stick to it I'm sure you won't be disappointed.

THE AIM OF THIS BOOK

A job done well always appears easy. This is certainly true of running marathons – except that the marathon has the potential for so many things to go wrong and wreck your plans. First you've got to survive the rigours of training without breaking down through illness or injury. Then, once you've got yourself to the start line, you have to negotiate your way around potential problems during the race. You might get a sidestitch at 10 miles or muscle cramp at the 20-mile point. At 15 miles you may find that you've drunk too much fluid, which is causing your stomach to churn around incessantly. You might be cruising along feeling fine with just six miles to the finish, only to find a few minutes later that you're on your knees as your last drops of energy drain away. You might end up running the last hour of the race suffering the agony of a blister every time your foot strikes the tarmac. Trying to eliminate these and other problems will increase your chances of success in the marathon. Helping you to do this is one of my motivations in writing this book.

I also wanted to write a book that went beyond a straightforward manual on marathon running. To do this I have tried to illustrate different aspects of marathon preparation and competition with reference to my own running experience. During the six years of my international marathon career (1993–98) and many more years before and since then, I have learned things from many people about training, race preparation and performance. This book gives me the opportunity to pass on what I have learned to others. Although in these more personal extracts my perspective is that of the elite competitor, my aim throughout has been to offer advice applicable to all levels of marathon runner, from the complete novice to the experienced competitor.

The book is divided into two sections. The first part, *What Every Runner Needs to Know*, starts out with the basics of designing a training routine, and goes on to examine the key areas of training and preparation for running your marathon. In the second part, *Aiming For The Top*, the advice is more relevant for those who already have a fair amount of running experience – although I hope that other runners might draw lessons from the topics too. Each chapter contains a *Key Points* section, which summarises the main learning points, followed by a *Useful Tips* section of relevant, additional advice. I then give an insight into my own marathon experience, reflecting on the topic under discussion. Outlines of training schedules relating to various aspects of marathon training are given throughout the book; these are further supplemented in the Appendices, which contain complete training programmes for the marathon, from the five-hour runner to those at elite – or sub-2:30 – level.

My main hope is that this book will help you achieve your goals in running your marathon. By the time you finish reading, most of those earlier questions about marathon running should have been answered – though I leave it to you to guess whether or not I'm a chocolate-eating marathon runner!

London Marathon participants enter the race's final mile

PART ONE

WHAT EVERY RUNNER NEEDS TO KNOW

*The start of Africa's biggest road race: more than
35,000 participants in Addis Ababa at the start of
the 2009 Great Ethiopian Run International 10km*

On the shores of Lake Hawassa in Ethiopia in one of the world's more scenic half-marathons

01

STARTING OUT

The aim of this chapter is to introduce you to a routine of training. You're more likely to get fit by being consistent with a manageable amount of training than by making heroic efforts which leave you worn out and dreading the arrival of your next workout. The secret is to be patient and enjoy seeing your fitness improve gradually over time.

GETTING INTO THE HABIT

Your first priority should be to start out gently and build up gradually. There's no need to think big yet. Learn to walk before you can jog; then combine some walking and jogging; then start to shift the balance towards doing more jogging than walking. Try to find a regular time of day to exercise. Maybe you'll want to get it done first thing in the morning before the rest of the family is up and about, or perhaps fit it into your lunch-hour at work. Fixing a regular time in the day to exercise will make it easier for people around you. Soon they will expect to see you putting on your running shoes at a certain point in the day; this in turn should help you stick to your resolve.

Having a training partner can be a great stimulus to training in these early days – especially when the initial enthusiasm has worn off and the last thing you feel like doing is going out for a training run. Try to arrange at least one session per week with a friend or group of fellow runners.

You should give yourself at least six weeks both to get used to a training routine and to see improvements in fitness, and ideally you should have followed this routine for at least three months before you start a marathon-training programme. During this period, set yourself achievable goals; enjoy the novelty of going out to exercise; and keep reminding yourself of the progress you have made since you first started.

Before you get going, have a look at the *Useful Tips* section on pp. 20–21. This offers some practical advice about how best to get started and stuck into a routine of training.

STRUCTURING YOUR TRAINING

If you're starting out as a running novice with a view to running a marathon, you will probably fall into one of two camps:

- the complete beginner, starting from scratch
- the first-time marathoner – someone who has done a fair amount of exercise, perhaps including some running, but with little experience of having followed a structured programme of running training.

For both groups, it's good to get into the habit of making one of your weekly sessions last for at least an hour – for most people this will be easiest at the weekend – since this session will become a key part of your training once you start your marathon build-up.

The warm-up and warm-down

A training session, as distinct from simply taking exercise, can be thought of as a three-stage process involving preparation, performance and recovery. Your training begins by ensuring that you are appropriately dressed (*see Useful Tips*, pp. 20–21) and warmed up (*see* below) – the 'preparation'

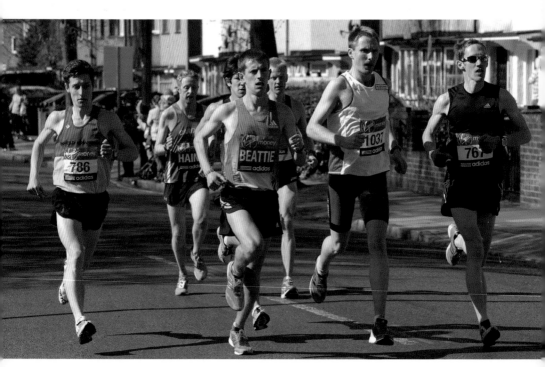

After running his first marathon in New York in 2011, John Beattie (centre) improved his best time by more than seven minutes to 2:16:38 in the 2012 London Marathon

Q&A SHOULD STRETCHING ALWAYS BE STATIC?

A comment frequently made about many Kenyan and Ethiopian runners is about the range of mobile stretching and loosening exercises – such as arm circling and leg kicking – performed in their warm-up and warm-down routines. Many of these exercises simulate the movement made during running. When learned properly from those familiar with such exercises, these routines can find a useful place in an athlete's overall conditioning programme, with the more static stretches being held over until the workout is finished and the athlete is relaxing back at home. The same applies for more 'rapid-fire' plyometric exercises which can guard against injury by strengthening certain muscle groups. Good advice from a coach is also required to ensure that these exercises are correctly learned and applied.

phase. The 'performance' component of training involves walking or running for a set amount of time or distance. This is followed by a period of recovery which should ideally include both refreshment (taking in food and drink, perhaps having a shower) and relaxation (stretching and rest).

When you go out for a walk or easy run, your warm-up and warm-down may consist simply of a short sequence of easy stretching exercises (*see* pp. 6–9). When you progress to doing some faster running, I recommend that you begin by doing 5–10 minutes of easy running, followed by some stretching, before starting the main part of your workout. In this way you will be reducing the 'shock effect' upon your body, which in turn reduces the risk of getting injured. Then for the warm-down at the end of your hard effort, repeat the process of easy jogging and stretching.

Following are some common stretching exercises to incorporate into your warm-up and warm-down routines.

STRETCHING FOR MARATHON RUNNERS

I have met very few runners who enjoy stretching, yet also very few who disagree with the view that stretching is an important way to stay free of injury. Recognising both these things, below are a set of seven stretches which could be incorporated into a short stretching routine either pre- or post-exercise, but ideally performed when your muscles are already warm, so if done before your run they could follow a short 5-minute warm-up jog.

For more detailed advice refer to an established book on the subject, such as *The Complete Guide to Stretching* by Christopher M. Norris (A & C Black)

CALVES

Lengthens and stretches the gastrocnemius and soleus muscles at the back of the lower leg.

Starting position

Stand facing a wall or post, in a 'half-lunge' position with your right foot forwards. Your feet should be parallel and about hip-width apart. Place your hands on the wall.

The stretch (gastrocnemius)

Push against the wall/post with your right (front) leg bent, and your back leg extended with the knee locked. Keep the heel of your back leg firmly on the ground throughout the stretch. Repeat on the other side. (This stretch can also be executed with both feet together as illustrated.)

The stretch (soleus)

Stand in the same starting position as for the gastrocnemius stretch, but bend your back knee slightly to alter the emphasis of the stretch to the lower calf.

QUADRICEPS (FRONT OF THIGHS)

Lengthens and stretches the quadriceps muscles at the front of the thigh. If the hips are tilted forwards, this will also stretch the hip flexors (*see* below).

Starting position and stretch

Standing on your left leg – using a wall or training partner for balance, if necessary – flex your right leg and grip the ankle with your right hand. Pull your heel towards the centre of your right buttock and hold (you can use your hand to increase the range of motion). Repeat on the other side. Throughout the stretch, ensure that your hips are facing forwards and avoid hollowing your lower back.

ADDUCTORS (INNER THIGHS)

Lengthens and stretches the adductor muscles, on the inside of the thigh.

Starting position and stretch

Sit with your back upright. Place the soles of your feet together and let your knees gently lower, until you obtain a comfortable stretch inside the thigh and groin. Either place your hands on the floor behind, to keep the spine upright, or press hands on the inside of your knees to increase the stretch. (An alternative is to straddle your legs out wide and straight, easing your legs apart with your hands by applying pressure on the inside of your knees.)

7

HAMSTRINGS (BACK OF THIGHS)

Lengthens and stretches the hamstring muscles at the back of the thigh.

Starting position and stretch

Stand with one leg resting on a bench at knee height. The knee should not be bent. Your standing leg should also be straight. Bend forwards from the hips towards the toes of your raised leg. Don't hunch your back; keep your chin up as you lean gently forwards. Repeat on the other side.

GLUTEALS (BUTTOCKS)

Lengthens and stretches the gluteal muscles in the buttocks.

Starting position and stretch

Either lie on the floor with your left leg straight, or sit on the floor with your back upright and your left leg extended out in front of you (as illustrated). Bend your right leg and cross it over your left, with your foot as close in to your body as is comfortably possible. Wrapping your left arm around your right leg as shown, 'hug' the knee into your body until you feel a stretch in your right buttock. Hold, then repeat on the other side.

ILIOPSOAS (HIP FLEXORS)

Lengthens and stretches the iliopsoas muscle, running through to the front of the femur (thigh bone) from the pelvis and lumbar spine.

Starting position and stretch

Kneel on the floor. Step your right leg forwards into a lunge position, with the foot flat on the floor. Keep the knee of your left leg on the floor. Press the hips forwards until you feel a stretch. You can rest your hands on your hips, on your right knee, or on the floor to help you keep your balance. Keep your chest 'lifted' and your back straight. Repeat on the other side.

Intensity/running type used in Tables 1.1 to 1.8 is best described as follows:

- **Brisk** – a quick running pace, but not sprinting
- **Easy** – as slowly as you like
- **Steady** – quicker than 'easy' but at a pace that still allows you to keep up a conversation with your training partner
- **Tempo** – as fast as you can sustain for the given time/distance
- **Strides** – running fast (feeling relaxed, not strained) over 100–120m

The first two weeks

Tables 1.1 and 1.2 detail what the first two weeks of training should look like for both the beginner and the first-time marathoner.

Note: the timing doesn't have to be exact, but it may help to glance at a watch in order to keep the proportions about right. You may find (for the one minute of brisk running) that you prefer to count strides – roughly 90 'right-foot-downs' at a brisk pace will take one minute. Alternatively, if you find yourself running on a street with lampposts, you could jog for three lampposts, and then run briskly for four or five, rather than timing yourself.

TABLE 1.1 WEEKS 1 AND 2 FOR THE BEGINNER

WEEK 1		WEEK 2	
Session 1	Walk 30 mins	**Session 1**	Walk 30 mins
Session 2	Walk 30 mins	**Session 2**	Walk 30 mins
Session 3	Walk 30 mins	**Session 3**	Walk 30 mins
Session 4	Long walk or cycle – at least 1hr	**Session 4**	Long walk or cycle – at least 1hr

VIEW FROM THE ROAD
Rosanna Bortoli

Rosanna Bortoli ran her first marathon in London in 2003 in a time of 5 hours and 36 minutes (which included a half-hour stop waiting outside a portaloo!)

I took up running quite by chance when I was on holiday in Italy a few years ago. I woke up early one morning and decided to walk and jog to the next village about four miles away – and I did it! I felt so good afterwards that I tried to do the same run every other day of the holiday. It sounds quite easy, but it was quite a big step for me because I'd never managed to stick to an exercise routine before and never imagined that I would enjoy running as much as I do. I'm also the type of person who doesn't plan ahead much, but with running it often doesn't require much forward planning. My friends and family were really supportive once they realised how much I enjoyed it, and now occasionally my son and daughter even come out running with me. A routine of training only really started when I committed to running the London Marathon for Mencap. And running did not stop when I had run my marathon. I still do one longish run at the weekend lasting about two hours, plus one or two other shorter runs in the week. I couldn't give up running now – in fact my body is very good at telling me that it needs exercise!

TABLE 1.2 WEEKS 1 AND 2 FOR THE FIRST-TIME MARATHONER

WEEK 1		WEEK 2	
Session 1	Easy run 20 mins	**Session 1**	Easy run 30 mins
Session 2	Easy run 30 mins	**Session 2**	10 mins easy run for warm-up, then 1 min brisk run, followed by 1 min jog. Repeat 5 times; 5 mins warm-down
Session 3	Easy run 20 mins	**Session 3**	Easy run 30 mins
Session 4	Run for 30 mins or long walk/cycle for at least 1.5hrs	**Session 4**	Run for 40 mins or long walk/cycle for at least 1.5hrs

The next two weeks

TABLE 1.3 WEEKS 3 AND 4 FOR THE BEGINNER

WEEK 3		WEEK 4	
Session 1	Walk 30 mins	**Session 1**	Walk 10 mins; next 10 mins, walk 1 min/jog 1 min × 5; walk 10 mins
Session 2	Walk 10 mins; next 10 mins, walk 1 min/jog 1 min × 5; walk 10 mins	**Session 2**	Walk 40 mins
Session 3	Walk 30 mins	**Session 3**	Walk 10 mins; walk 90 secs/jog 90 secs × 2; walk 1 min/jog 1 min × 4; walk 10 mins
Session 4	Long walk/cycle for at least 1hr	**Session 4**	Long walk/cycle for at least 1hr

Note: if you find it pretty tough to jog for one full minute (see Week 3, Session 2), jog for about 100 m, then walk until you get your breath back again. An easier alternative to the walk/jog routine is easy walking/brisk walking.

TABLE 1.4 WEEKS 3 AND 4 FOR THE FIRST-TIME MARATHONER

WEEK 3		WEEK 4	
Session 1	Easy run 30 mins	Session 1	Easy run 30 mins
Session 2	Easy run 15 mins; steady run 15 mins	Session 2	Warm-up 10 mins easy run; 2 mins steady run/ 2 mins jog
Session 3	Easy run 30 mins	Session 3	Easy run 30 mins
Session 4	45 mins run or long walk/ cycle for 1.5hrs	Session 4	45 mins run or long walk/ cycle for 1.5hrs

The second month
The beginner
If you have built up gradually according to the schedules above, you should now feel confident to jog for two minutes at one stretch. Over the next few weeks you should aim to include as much jogging in your walk/jog sessions as possible without exhausting yourself. Keep in one walking-only session, and one longer session.

TABLE 1.5 THE SECOND MONTH FOR BEGINNERS

WEEKS 5 & 7		WEEKS 6 & 8	
Session 1	Walk/jog 30 mins	Session 1	Easy run 30 mins
Session 2	Walk 5 mins; walk 2 mins/jog 2 mins × 5 (week 5) or walk 2 mins/jog 3 mins × 4 (week 7); walk 5 mins	Session 2	Jog 10 mins/walk 5 mins/jog 10 mins in week 6; in week 8 try a continuous jog for 20 mins – go on, surprise yourself!
Session 3	Walk 30–40 mins	Session 3	Walk 30–40 mins
Session 4	Long walk/cycle for at least 1hr	Session 4	Long walk/cycle for at least 1hr

COMMITTING TO A ROUTINE OF TRAINING

As easy as it may be to prescribe ways of getting into a routine of training, the reality is that it's not so easy in practice. Instead of giving my own prescriptions, below are several 'first-hand' tips from those who have recently taken up running and successfully managed to get into a routine of regular training.

- 'As soon as I get home from work I put on my running gear. I don't sit down or stop for a cup of tea, because I know that this might make me think about putting it off. It also helps if I have arranged to run with a friend after work.'
- 'I like to mix my running routes so I don't get bored of running in the same places. It gives me different things to look forward to as I go through the week. Sometimes I simply run one of my usual routes in the opposite direction. I also change my speeds and the distances I run. For me, routine is all about variety.'
- 'I make sure that I have a substantial lunch at work so that I can do my training straight after work. Morning workouts leave my legs too tired for my job which involves a lot of time on my feet.'
- 'At the weekend I prefer running in the morning, so it's not hanging over me for the rest of the day. I try to fall out of bed straight into my running clothes.'
- 'Where I run matters a lot to me. The thought of being outside at one with nature is enough to get me out running.'
- 'I like to fit in my running early in the morning. It's tough getting up early on a cold morning, but sometimes it's even harder declining a drink with colleagues after work in order to get out for a run.'
- 'Committing to a routine of training is not just about sticking rigidly to a set programme; for me, it's about enjoying my running and being part of a running group where I can encourage others and be encouraged by them. I also get a lot out of taking part in races, giving me goals to aim for.'

The first-time marathoner

By the end of your first month of training, you will be doing at least two hours of running per week. Your aim over the next month is to increase gradually the total amount of running (up to three hours by the end of the second month) while introducing some quicker running once or twice a week. Remember to respect the meaning of 'steady running' – it means making more of an effort than an easy jog, but still staying well below maximal effort.

TABLE 1.6 THE SECOND MONTH FOR THE FIRST-TIME MARATHONER

WEEKS 5 & 7		WEEKS 6 & 8	
Session 1	Easy run 10 mins; steady run 10 mins × 2	**Session 1**	Steady run 30 mins (week 6) or steady run 40 mins (week 8)
Session 2	Easy run 30 mins	**Session 2**	Easy run 40 mins
Session 3	Warm-up 10 mins easy run; 1 min brisk run/1 min jog × 10; warm-down 5 mins	**Session 3**	Warm-up 10 mins easy run; 4 mins steady run/4 mins jog, then 3/3, 2/2 and 1/1; warm-down 5 mins. In week 8, do 5/5, 4/4, 3/3, 2/2 and 1/1 for steady run/jog sets
Session 4	Run 50 mins (week 5) or 55 mins (week 7), or long walk/cycle for 2hrs	**Session 4**	Run 50 mins (week 6) or 60 mins (week 8), or long walk/cycle for 2hrs

Entering your third month of training

You should be starting to feel much fitter now than when you started. As you continue to increase your training, listen carefully to any 'warning signs' from your body that you might be overdoing it. If you're particularly tired one day, don't be afraid to take a day off. You should also resist the temptation to time yourself over the same routes – vary the places and routes for your training runs (*see* also p. 20).

Here's your training plan for Weeks 9–12 of a three-month preparation period getting you into the routine of training.

TABLE 1.7 WEEKS 9–12 FOR THE BEGINNER

WEEKS 9 & 10		WEEKS 11 & 12	
Session 1	Walk/jog 30 mins	Session 1	Jog for 20–25 mins (week 11) 25–30 mins (week 12)
Session 2	Jog 10 mins/walk 5 mins/ jog 10 mins (week 9) or jog 20 mins (week 10)	Session 2	Jog for 20–25 mins (week 11) 25–30 mins (week 12)
Session 3	Walk/jog 30 mins	Session 3	Jog/walk 35 mins or jog 20 mins
Session 4	Long walk/jog 45–50 mins (try to jog as much as possible, but don't be afraid to walk, particularly up hills)	Session 4	Long walk/jog 45–50 mins (as session 4 for weeks 9 and 10)

TABLE 1.8 WEEKS 9–12 FOR THE FIRST-TIME MARATHONER

WEEK 9		WEEK 10	
Session 1	Easy run 10 mins/brisk run 5 mins/easy run 5 mins; warm-down 10 mins	Session 1	Easy run 10 mins; brisk run 2 mins/jog 2 mins × 6; easy run 10 mins
Session 2	Steady run 40 mins	Session 2	Steady run 40 mins
Session 3	Jog 1 min/brisk run 1 min, then 2/2, 3/3, 4/4, 3/3, 2/2, 1/1 (commonly known as a 'pyramid' session)	Session 3	Warm-up 5 mins; steady run 2 mins/easy run 2 mins × 6; warm-down 5 mins
Session 4	Long run 60 mins	Session 4	Long run 65 mins

TABLE 1.8 WEEKS 9–12 FOR THE FIRST-TIME MARATHONER cont.

WEEK 11		WEEK 12	
Session 1	Easy run 10 mins; tempo run 15 mins; easy run 10 mins	**Session 1**	Warm-up 10 mins; 1 min running fast uphill/recovery jog downhill × 10; warm-down 10 mins
Session 2	Steady run 45 mins	**Session 2**	Steady run 45 mins
Session 3	Easy run 30 mins; 100 m strides × 8	**Session 3**	Warm-up 5 mins; easy run 1 min/steady run 1 min, then 2/2, 3/3, 4/4, 3/3, 2/2, 1/1 (pyramid session); warm-down 5 mins
Session 4	Long run 65 mins	**Session 4**	Long run 70 mins

A local fun run is a good event to run your first race, where just participating with others is more important than what you are wearing or how fast you run

EXPERT COMMENT
Steven Seaton: Getting Started for a Marathon

Steven Seaton, former editor of *Runner's World* magazine and now Publishing Director at Hearst Magazines

The hardest thing about training for a marathon is the time you have to commit to it. If you are used to runs of 30 to 40 minutes three times a week, then suddenly picking that up to four, five or six runs a week, each lasting 60 minutes or longer, requires a tremendous commitment. But there are no shortcuts; the marathon is an honest distance, and you reap on race day what you sow in training. If there is one element you should focus on, make it the long run – that, above all else, will dictate the success or failure of your first marathon. A reasonably fit person could build up to a marathon from nothing in four months. Six months would be better, but if you are coming from a good fitness base as little as three months would suffice. You don't need a coach or a running club to achieve your marathon goals – although they would help – because you, and you alone, are the key to a successful marathon.

RUNNING YOUR FIRST RACE

By the end of your third month of regular training, you should be ready to enter your first competition. The thought of racing might fill you with dread, but if you're thinking of running a marathon at some future date, you've got to start somewhere. Besides, running a race will give you some idea of how your training is going. A local 5km or 10km race is probably the best place to start. Don't be afraid of being left behind: you'll meet plenty of runners like yourself whose main ambition is not to run a quick time, but simply to get around.

If you plan to do a race at the end of Week 13, your final week of training before the race should look something like this.

TABLE 1.9 PRE-RACE TRAINING FOR THE BEGINNER

WEEK 13	
Session 1	Jog 8 mins/walk 2 mins × 3
Session 2	Jog 20 mins
Session 3	Have a rest day!
Session 4	5km or 10km race

TABLE 1.10 PRE-RACE TRAINING FOR THE FIRST-TIME MARATHONER

WEEK 13	
Session 1	Warm-up 5 mins; tempo 5 mins/jog 3 mins × 3; warm-down 5 mins
Session 2	Steady run 30 mins
Session 3	Have a rest day!
Session 4	5 mile or 10km race

If you have completed the programme above for your first three months of training, you will be in a much better position to embark on a marathon-training programme than when you first started out. You're now up and running, and ready to move on to the marathon build-up for real!

KEY POINTS
- Consider carefully how best to fit exercise into your daily routine
- Don't be over-ambitious: set yourself achievable goals
- Aim for consistency in training; the key to improving fitness over time
- Vary your training routes, and if possible run on soft surfaces
- Don't always time yourself; go further not faster
- Be flexible and prepared to modify your training programme if need be.

'There's no such thing as bad weather, only inappropriate clothing': training with Kenyan runners in Colorado in 1996

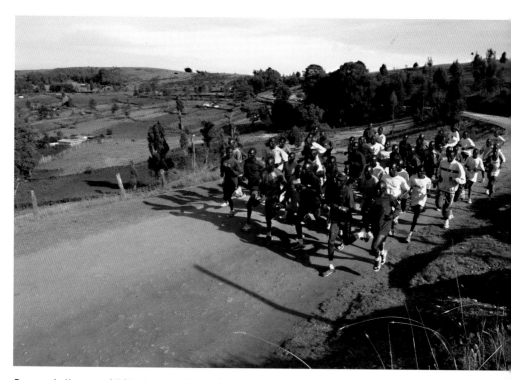

Runners in Kenya and Ethiopia are well known for training in large groups

VIEW FROM THE ROAD
James Pinto

James Pinto ran his debut marathon in Brighton in 2011
Preparing for my first marathon was a step into the unknown. When I signed up, I had run a few half marathons but nothing close to 26.2 miles. To help me get serious, I decided one year before doing the marathon to join a local running club. This got me out running at least once a week and gave me the chance to ask more experienced runners for tips on training. With six months to go, I started running at least three times a week. Basing my training on what I had learned, I tried to do one longer run each week and increase the duration of this run as the marathon got closer. My longest run was just short of 2.5 hours. On race day I was pretty nervous. It was a warm day and I wasn't sure how my body would cope after 2 hours. In the end I got round in 4:17. I felt a great sense of achievement in reaching the finish line.

USEFUL TIPS: GETTING STARTED

What do I wear?

Good supportive running shoes – not just your old pair of trainers that you used to play tennis in at school. Get a pair of shoes that are generous when your feet are at 'room temperature', as they will expand a bit as you run. Depending on the weather, you should exercise in a loose T-shirt and long tights or tracksuit bottoms (or shorts if you feel more comfortable in these). Women may want to buy a good sports bra from a department store or sports shop.

How fast should I run?

At a pace that is relaxed and comfortable. Initially this may be just a walk, but soon you should be able to combine this with a short jog (*see* training schedules, pp. 9–12). If you have a training partner, you should exercise at a pace which allows you to talk. Remember, in these early stages it's better to go further than faster.

Where should I run?

Preferably away from busy streets, but if you are running in the dark then it's better to stay on well-lit routes. Ideally you should do some of your running off-road, perhaps in a nearby park or along some dirt trails: your legs suffer less pounding on softer surfaces and your surroundings will make you feel more at ease. It's also good to vary your routes. If you always complete the same circuit, it's easy to get into the habit of racing yourself over the distance. You can do this once every two weeks perhaps, but not every day.

Q&A: HOW DO I FIND THE RIGHT SHOES?

Haile Gebrselassie once commented that one reason his hero Abebe Bekila ran in bare feet was that the alternatives at the time were poor and limited. Today we have lots of choice and far superior running shoe technology. The best place to start is in a specialist running store where you should be able to get good advice on what shoes are best for you. Apart from price, you should first think about comfort and cushioning. You might also have the luxury of an in-store gait analysis (see p. 58) where your running action on a treadmill can be analysed by computer and advice given accordingly.

How can I reduce the risk of breakdown through illness or injury?
By warming up, properly, stretching well (*see* pp. 5–9) and giving your body
time to recover from strenuous bouts of exercise. Give your body a chance to
warm up, too, by progressing either from a walk to a jog or (if you're fitter)
from an easy jog to a run – it does little good, and may even cause you an
injury, if you sprint off from the start. Stretching post-exercise, in particular
for the calves, hamstrings and quadriceps, will help guard against acute
feelings of stiffness. If you have time and opportunity, have a swim or sauna
– ideal for tired muscles after a run. Rest should also be seen as an important
component of training, so that you don't wear yourself out completely. Just
because things appear to be going well, don't do too much too soon. Finally,
use the training schedules sensibly and be prepared to modify them according
to your lifestyle.

(For women) Can I run when I have my period?
Yes, running may even help ease the discomfort through the release of pain-
relieving endorphins.

Should I change my diet?
Your running will benefit if you are eating a healthy, well balanced diet:
lots of fruit and vegetables, a good supply of carbohydrate-rich food and
sufficient protein (*see* Chapter 4 for more detail). Fatty foods should be kept
to a minimum. Make sure too that you keep adequately hydrated; for every
20 minutes of running you should drink about 300ml of fluid, and drink more
when training in hot conditions. Whatever time of day you exercise, it's good
to take some food and drink soon after finishing. Eating and drinking sensibly
will help you to recover more quickly from the exertions of training.

Where can I get more advice?
Today there is a proliferation of websites and runner's blogs with information
about how to train for the marathon, specific programmes and first-hand
advice. If you prefer magazines, *Runner's World*, *Men's Running* and *Women's
Running* offer all kinds of ideas and advice on matters such as how to get the
most out of your training, overcome injury and improve your diet. You will
also find useful updates on the latest shoe models and items of sportswear,
and motivational stories about runners who once started out just as you are
now doing.

VIEW FROM THE ROAD
Nigel Wilson: How I took up running

Nigel Wilson could not resist the appeal of running the London Marathon. He achieved his goal in a time of 4 hours and 15 minutes
I took up running for the sole purpose of running the London Marathon. Having watched the race over the years on the television and live from the streets, it had become an ambition to take part and to try to achieve those 26 miles. I was physically fit when I started training – since my schooldays, swimming training had always been a regular feature in my life – but I was no sort of runner. At the start, running just for ten minutes was a big effort, but quite soon it built up to half an hour, and then, within a couple of months of starting to train, up to one-hour runs. Like many first-timers, I started my training for London in the New Year and somehow managed to complete the 26 miles three months later. I stopped running almost immediately afterwards. I now do some running as part of my general fitness, but never for more than 20 minutes at a time.

BECOMING A MARATHON RUNNER
HAMBURG, MAY 1993

In April 1985, midway through my undergraduate course at Oxford University, I was selected to represent a combined Oxford–Cambridge athletics team on a tour to compete against the Ivy League colleges in the USA. On one of our rest days after a competition in Providence, Rhode Island, we were given the option of going to the beach in Newport or going to watch the Boston Marathon. For the distance runners on the team, it was an easy decision to make. This was one of the world's most famous marathons, with a history that went back to the start of the modern Olympics. It would also be my first opportunity to witness a marathon 'in the flesh'. Soon we were on the road, heading north up I-95 towards Boston.

MY FIRST MARATHON EXPERIENCE
By the time we parked the car at the 22-mile point at Cleveland Circle, word had reached us that the pre-race favourite, Geoff Smith from England, had gone off like a madman, passing through 10km at world-record pace in 29:05. We ran over to a local bar on the corner of Cleveland Circle, where the television screen showed Smith going further and further away from the rest of the field. He was attacking Steve Jones's recent world-best mark of 2:08:05 for the marathon. Excitement grew as Smith reached 20 miles still on schedule to set a new world best. Then suddenly, as we watched on the screen, disaster struck. He stopped and clasped his hamstrings. He walked a bit, then started jogging. He covered the 21st mile in over six minutes. By the time he came past us, he was doing all he could just to keep going. His earlier serious demeanour had turned to one of disbelief. At this point, Smith was still over a mile ahead of the second-placed runner. Somehow he managed to claw his way to the finish in a time of 2:14:05, six minutes outside Jones's record, but still with a winning margin of over five minutes. We left Boston that afternoon having learned how cruel and unforgiving an event the marathon can be.

MAKING PROGRESS
In my final year as a student, I finally made a breakthrough into big-time athletics by gaining selection to compete on the British team at the 1989 World Cross-Country Championships in Norway. Led home by Tim Hutchings, who won the individual silver, the British team finished second behind Kenya. I was 49th. And so, at the age of 25, my international career was underway. I was dubbed a late developer, though I had actually been running seriously

for over 15 years. At the age of nine I had won a bag of crisps for breaking the record in the school race. Now I was gaining international honours.

In my years as a schoolboy and then student runner I had enjoyed some success, but I was still some way off being among the very best. Why had I kept at it for so long, if success alone had not been the sole motivating factor? I was still running because it was something I enjoyed. I enjoyed the fun of running with others. I enjoyed the feeling of well-being it gave me. I enjoyed, too, the challenges it provided. And I enjoyed the satisfaction of doing well and improving at it, even when I was not winning. By now, running had become part of my identity.

STEPPING STONES TO MY FIRST MARATHON

Three years later, after a disappointing 17th place finish in the 10,000m final in the 1992 Barcelona Olympics, I took an end-of-season break. At the beginning of October, I started to plan out my training for the winter leading up to my first marathon – scheduled for the following spring. It had long been my intention to move up from the 10,000m to the marathon. I was now 29 years old, and thus at a stage of my development when I was both physically and mentally strong enough to master the distance. While I still had a number of years of my international career ahead of me, I wanted to start gaining experience at the marathon. If things went to plan, I hoped to reach my peak in time for the next Olympics in Atlanta.

My coach, Bruce Tulloh, was keen for me not to make any drastic changes to the training that had served me so well for the past few years. As a 10,000m runner I was already running a high weekly mileage, so moving up to the marathon only required a slight shift of emphasis towards greater endurance, and this could be introduced gradually over the course of the winter. In fact, for most of the autumn I stuck with my familiar routine, which included lots of good aerobic running and a number of good 10km workouts designed to improve my speed. The only slight changes were an increase in the duration of my long endurance run at the weekend, and the introduction of more regular interval workouts on the road, run over longer distances at a more controlled pace. Even though I wasn't yet into a marathon build-up for real, Bruce was already keen for me to start shifting my thinking towards the event.

The winter got off to a good start when I ran a personal best for the half-marathon of 1:01:33 in Orlando, Florida in early December. It looked as though I was well on target for a promising debut. But in February 1993 I picked up an illness that forced me to withdraw from the British team for the World Cross-Country Championships, the first time I had missed the event since 1989. The virus prevented me from resuming normal training until the last week of March, leaving me little time to prepare for my debut marathon, originally planned for the first weekend of May. From all the good training

I had done since the previous summer I knew I had the background to run a good marathon; but at the same time I realised there was no need to rush my marathon build-up. In view of this, I decided to postpone the date of my debut marathon by three weeks, and set myself the task of preparing for the Hamburg Marathon on 23 May 1993.

LOW-KEY APPROACH

I went into my first marathon deliberately trying not to put any pressure on myself. The fact that I had only recently recovered from my illness – thus curtailing the length of my build-up – also helped to ensure that I had modest ambitions this time around.

My aim was to get a feel for the distance – not to break any records. I wanted to come out of the race with a positive first experience. If I was serious about embarking on a career as a marathon runner, it made more sense to be cautious than over-ambitious. It would certainly do my confidence no good to blow up disastrously, or even worse, fail to finish at my first attempt.

My plan was to run at an even pace for the entire distance. I then had to determine what time I should aim for at the halfway point. The previous autumn I had run 1:01:33 for the half-marathon; and three weeks before my debut in Hamburg, I had run 1:02:39 on an undulating course in Exeter. On this basis I reckoned that I should be able to reach halfway in the marathon in around 66 minutes without feeling too tired, and then aim to finish in around 2:12.

PRE-RACE ARRANGEMENTS

I flew out to Hamburg two days before the race. I knew the city well from my student days, when I had worked in Europe as a bus tour guide, so I was already able to picture parts of the marathon route from the course map which I had received before leaving home. Bruce, his wife Sue and my mother – my three most stalwart supporters throughout my athletic career – flew out with me, and we were soon checked into our hotel, situated less than a five-minute jog from the start and finish of the course in the centre of Hamburg.

On the day before the race there were a few matters to attend to. First, we were driven around the course by the race organisers. Then, there was a technical meeting at which all the final pre-race details – such as arrangements for the special drinks stations – were given out. The weather was predicted to be cool with a slight breeze.

In an attempt to beat the existing course record of 2:10:43, we were told that the intended pace of the leaders for the first half of the race would be 1:05:00. This meant that I would have to restrain myself from going off with the leaders, since I had deliberately set myself a more conservative halfway target of 1:06:00.

In the morning, and again in the early evening, I did an easy 20-minute run which took in the last 2km of the course – on the basis that it's far more important to know how the race finishes than how it starts. The remainder of my pre-race day was spent relaxing with my feet up in my hotel bedroom, while my supporters familiarised themselves with the transport system that they would be using the following day to get around the course.

My debut in Hamburg had received relatively little pre-race coverage in the athletics media, which helped to take the pressure off me. David Powell, athletics correspondent for *The Times*, was the only journalist who had travelled out to Hamburg to report on the race. On the evening before the race we met up with him in the hotel, and the five of us went out for a pasta meal together.

RACE DAY IN HAMBURG

An hour before the race began, I walked the short distance to the start with Bruce. My legs were feeling loose even before starting my warm-up, so I held myself back from doing too much running prior to the start of the race. I jogged easily for five minutes, did some stretching, jogged for another five minutes, and did a few strides. Just before 9.00a.m. we were called to the elite start, and the race got underway. My main point of focus in the early few miles was not to run too fast; I had no intention of charging off at the pace of the leaders. Glancing at my watch after the first kilometre, I realised that I had run slower than intended (3:14 min/km as opposed to my target pace of 3:07), so slightly raised my tempo for the next few miles. At the first drinks station after 5km, race officials were trying to help the runners by handing them their special drinks. However, they had failed to pick up my bottle, so I virtually had to stop and push my way through to find it. At this stage of the race, refuelling was more important than a few seconds lost. From then on, I gradually worked to get back on to my pre-race schedule, passing the 10km point in 31:12. The leaders were by now out of sight, and I was running on my own.

I kept reminding myself to stay relaxed and conserve my effort for later in the race. Soon after the 15km drinks station I started to get a stitch, possibly from having drunk too much fluid at the first three stations, so I decided not to take my bottle at the next station. At 20km I quickly started to gain on a group of runners whom I then passed at the halfway stage (1:05:53). Unbeknown to me, the leaders were over a minute up on me at this point, having run 1:04:40 for the first half of the race. At 25km I still felt relaxed, though I was now running faster than at the start of the race. The Belorussian Vladimir Kotov ran behind me for a couple of kilometres, but by 28km I was again running on my own. Bruce called out to me that I was in fifth place, about 30 seconds down on the leaders. At 30km the lead car came into view. Soon I passed the fourth-placed runner, and within a further 2km I had caught up the two race leaders. With six miles of the race to go, I stopped thinking about pace and started thinking about how I might win the race.

For the next 5km I ran a few strides behind the two race leaders. Though we were still running quite fast (3:06 min/km), it felt much easier because I was now following rather than setting the pace. I gathered my strength to make a decisive attack. At the 23-mile point I surged ahead of the two African runners, and from then on continued to extend my lead. I came into the finish 41 seconds clear of the second-placed runner, Thomas Naali of Tanzania. My winning time was 2:10:57. I had run the second half of the race in 1:05:04, almost 50 seconds faster than the first half.

This had been a great start to my marathon career. In terms of my finishing time, I had comfortably achieved my goal, and done this by running faster over the second half of the course than over the first. My time was only seven seconds slower than Eamonn Martin's winning time in London a month previously. Winning the race had been a bonus.

POSTSCRIPT

Six hours after breasting the tape to complete my first marathon, I found myself staggering through the concourse at Hamburg airport. It had been a long day since our pre-race breakfast at 5.50a.m. Satisfaction with my performance, coupled with relief that the task had been accomplished, could not disguise an acute feeling of post-race weariness. My feet were still hot from pounding over 26 miles of tarmac. I had one or two nasty blisters. Bruce helped me by carrying my trophy, Sue held the bouquet of flowers. We had to return to London that evening, because on the following morning I was due to fly off to St. Petersburg in connection with some work I was doing for a church agency – and my flight to Russia was leaving at 6.55a.m. If it was true that I had played down my ambitions before the race, it was also the case that I had underestimated quite how tired I would be feeling afterwards.

My induction into the world of marathon racing had been a successful one. After many years of watching the event, I had at last experienced one for myself. Admittedly, the goals for my first marathon had been relatively modest; though after the uncertainties caused by my virus this seemed only right for my first attempt at the distance. Bruce and I felt there was much more to come and we had already started to map out the route ahead. We both felt excited about my future career as a marathon runner.

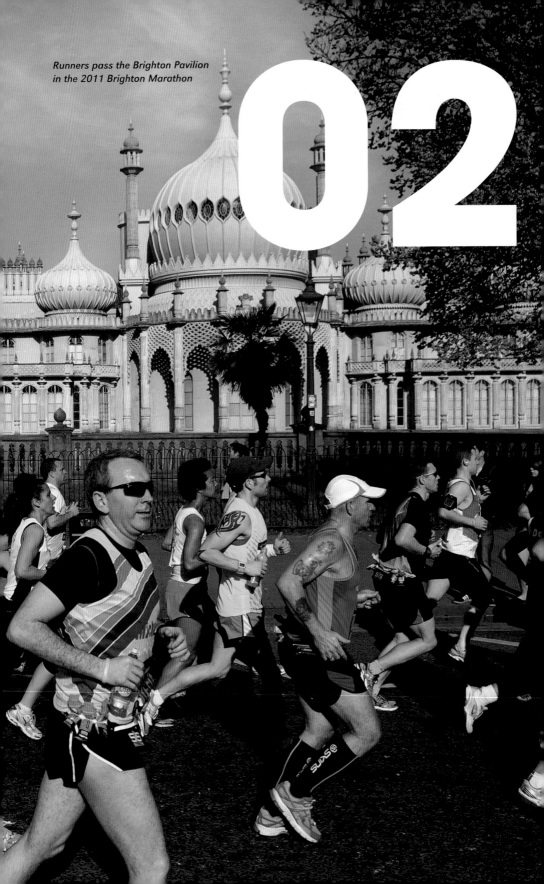

Runners pass the Brighton Pavilion in the 2011 Brighton Marathon

02

THE MARATHON BUILD-UP

How long do you need to prepare for a marathon? If you are starting from scratch, you should ideally give yourself at least a year of regular training before even thinking about running a marathon. During this period you can gradually extend the distance of your longer runs, as well as the total number of runs and miles that you are doing each week. Your first major goal towards the end of this period should be to run a half-marathon, and when you've achieved this you can then start to set your sights on running the full 26-mile distance.

The longer your preparatory period of developing fitness, the more confident you will feel when you come to think specifically about training for a marathon. The minimum length of preparation that I advocate for the first-time marathon runner is the three-month period outlined in Chapter 1. Thereafter the build-up itself – the period of marathon-specific training – should last a further three to four months. (Its exact length will depend on your running experience and your level of fitness.)

Table 2.1 is designed to help you – as a first-time marathoner – assess your readiness to embark on a three-month marathon build-up, relative to your goals. The key point here is not to stick rigidly to the figures shown, but to set your goals for your marathon according to the level of running that you have attained before starting your marathon build-up.

More advanced runners may be interested to see how I determined the length of my marathon build-ups based on my fitness level immediately beforehand (*see* Table 2.2). Note how my build-up periods were sometimes shorter than three months, simply because I already had a good base of endurance from the preceding block of training. When the pre-marathon period included more racing and a reduction in the volume of training (as in the autumn of 1993), I used a full 12-week build-up.

TABLE 2.1 ASSESSING YOUR READINESS FOR A THREE-MONTH BUILD-UP AS A FIRST-TIME MARATHONER

Marathon goals	Regular training before build-up	Volume of weekly running	Previous race experience
Complete the distance	3 months minimum	15 miles per week	5-10km
Less than 4.5hrs	3-6 months	25 miles per week	Half-marathon
Less than 4hrs	6-12 months	25-30 miles per week	Half-marathon in less than 2hrs
Less than 3.5hrs	12 months +	35 miles per week	10km in less than 44 mins*; half-marathon in less than 1hr 40 mins*

* These times differ both between and among male and female runners, so are only an approximate guide. In general, female runners aspiring to these goals should be further under this upper limit than male runners.

TABLE 2.2 DETERMINING THE LENGTH OF THE MARATHON BUILD-UP

Pre-build-up phase	Level of fitness at start of build-up	Length of build-up	Event and date
10,000m track race, followed by 3 weeks at altitude, 2 more track races, then one easy week	Good 5km track speed but short of endurance	12 weeks	San Sebastian, October 1993
8 weeks of track training and racing, finishing with	Good base of endurance after 10km training	10 weeks	Helsinki, August 1994
3 weeks at altitude, then one easy week followed by 2 cross-country races	Still enjoying benefits of good training at altitude	10 weeks	London, April 1997

Q&A FROM WHAT AGE SHOULD CHILDREN RUN A MARATHON?

The usual minimum age limit of 18 appears to be a sensible benchmark, even though there are many examples – including that of Haile Gebrselassie who ran his first marathon at the age of 15 – of younger children successfully completing marathon races. Probably the most important thing about children running long distances at an early age is that they should not be pushed into it by their parents or coaches, either in terms of the competition or what might normally be expected in terms of required training.

VIEW FROM THE ROAD
Karen Weir

Karen Weir loves the challenge of the marathon
What I love about the marathon is the challenge it gives me. It's big enough that you have to be serious about your training; but it's not too big that it's out of reach of ordinary folks like me. Once you're out on the road, it doesn't matter who you are or where you come from – it's simply about having the strength of body and mind to get round. I got hooked on marathons as soon as I ran my first one, which I did in 4:44. Now almost every year when January arrives I start my marathon training, for 12 to 16 weeks, leading up to a spring marathon. My time is now down to 3:36 and I'm still looking to get faster.

CHOOSING YOUR NEXT MARATHON

How should you go about deciding where to run a marathon? Aside from knowing the date of the race, it's useful to find out about the process of applying for a race entry, about your chances of getting a place and about the costs involved. Many of the big and better-known races are now either heavily over-subscribed (e.g. London) or expensive to enter (e.g. New York).

For the majority of British runners like Jane Thomson (see her View from the Road on p. 86) if you were to do just one marathon, London is still the 'must-do' race. However, your chances of getting a place through the lottery system are slim; if you are unsuccessful in the lottery, you have the option of securing a guaranteed place from a charity through the Golden Bond scheme. The vast majority of London Marathon participants do indeed end up running for charity, but don't take lightly the effort involved in raising the minimum amount to donate back to the charity.

Other important considerations for choosing a marathon are the weather conditions, the time of year when you will be doing the hardest period of your training, the ease and expense for yourself and your supporters of travelling to and staying at the event and the overall level of services provided for race participants.

Most marathon organisers work hard to ensure that their courses are as flat and fast as possible. The obvious exceptions are those marathons that sell themselves as scenic alternatives to the big-city races (e.g. the off-road Kielder Marathon in Northumberland and the Loch Ness Marathon in the Scottish Highlands).

Weather and destination are important particularly if you're likely to struggle in warm conditions or at the end of a long air journey across a number of time zones. Even though the main marathon seasons fall in the spring and autumn when the chances of encountering extreme heat or extreme cold are less, over the years certain races have gained a reputation for good marathon weather (e.g. Berlin), while others have seen unpredictable swings in temperature and climate on the day of the race (e.g. Boston and Chicago).

A large number of runners share the view of Karen Weir (see View from the Road, p. 31) and enjoy training for a marathon during the winter months leading towards a spring marathon, even though in Britain this means coping with colder weather and shorter hours of daylight for the bulk of your training. Not only are there a range of April marathon choices in Britain (Brighton, Milton Keynes and Manchester are currently among the alternatives to London) but March is also packed with popular half-marathon races up and down the country which serve as useful preparation races for the full distance. The preference for running a spring marathon also arises because many runners find it easier sticking to a routine in the first three months of the year than during the summer months.

With a greater number of marathons to choose from, competition for offering a superior level of service to participants is on the increase. It's worth finding out about the arrangements provided to participants such as the process for collecting your race number and arriving in the right start area, toilet and baggage facilities at the start, water stations along the route, signs on the course, distribution of medals at the finish and the results system. Either ask someone you know who has first-hand experience of the race or refer to some of the participant surveys conducted by the better-known running publications and websites.

Ultimately, your decision comes down to personal preference. Training for and completing a marathon is a big commitment so you need to think carefully about the date and type of marathon that will most help you stay motivated to train and focussed on your goal.

STRUCTURING A 12-WEEK BUILD-UP

The great thing about running training is that you can often start to see returns on your hard efforts within quite a short space of time. Within a six-week period, many runners can notice substantial gains in fitness. However, the art of successful training is to make small, gradual increases in your training loads from one week to the next, rather than to let your enthusiasm get the better of you and build up too hastily. An over-hasty start can not only lead to you flagging halfway through the build-up; it may also lead to injury and breakdown. Better to plan your training so that your body hardly notices the slight increases in training as you start to get fitter and progress towards your goal.

One useful way of viewing the overall pattern of a marathon-training programme is to divide your 12-week build-up into four quarters of three weeks each. As you progress from one quarter to the next, you gradually increase the volume and intensity of your training, so that by the third quarter you should be training at your hardest. Think of the four phases of your build-up as 'training well' (first phase); 'training hard' (second phase); 'training very hard' (third phase); and 'easing down and preparing to compete' (fourth phase). The final quarter is when you gradually start to reduce the amount of training and prepare to perform at your best in the race itself. Table 2.3 provides an example of this graduated approach to training loads over the course of a marathon build-up.

The length of your weekly long run should increase by small increments during each phase of the build-up (here, a three-week period) as well as from one phase to the next (as Table 2.3 shows). For those running up to 40 miles per week, total weekly mileage should increase by no more than 20 per cent from one week to the next; for those running more than 40 miles per week, the increase should be no more than 10 per cent from one week to the next. The merit of planning out the overall structure of your training in this way is that you learn to retain your enthusiasm and determination to train hard for when it is most needed – a skill that will also serve you well when it comes to running the marathon itself.

Note how the hardest phase of the training takes place once you are into the second half of the build-up. Structuring your training in this way will improve your chances of staying healthy and free of injury. The human body has an amazing capacity to adapt to new stresses placed upon it, but to allow it to do this you must be sensible in introducing those new stresses gradually. Too much stress at any one time will lead to breakdown.

TABLE 2.3

Training unit	Level	1st quarter	2nd quarter	3rd quarter	4th quarter
Weekly long run (miles)	Marathon novice	10–13	14–17	18–20	less than 15
	Advanced (less than 3hrs)	13–16	17–20	21–24	less than 18
Total weekly mileage	Marathon novice	20–30	30–40	40–50	less than 40
	Advanced (less than 3hrs)	50–60	60–70	70–80	less than 60

STUART'S STORY

Just before Christmas, Stuart was one of over 30,000 runners around the country who received a letter telling them that their entry had been accepted to run in the London Marathon the following April. For the past two years Stuart's application through the lottery had been rejected, so he was overjoyed to get his acceptance letter this time around. Having started running just over two years ago, and having competed in a number of local 10km road races, at last this was his chance to see how fast he could cover the 26-mile distance. With a lot of hard training and a bit of luck, he thought, maybe he could realise his ambition of running a marathon. He even set himself the challenge of breaking the four-hour barrier.

After sending off his entry in October, Stuart hadn't held out high hopes of having his entry accepted. In fact, as the autumn progressed he had got out of his regular routine of training and felt that he was slowly losing fitness. When news of his acceptance came through, he resolved to get serious again about his running once the Christmas festivities were over.

January 1 came around and he started the New Year with a long run to his wife's parents that took him over 1½ hours, longer than any run he had done previously by almost 20 minutes. The following week he was out running regularly on the dark, icy roads around his home, and had planned a route for his long run the following weekend. Soon he was beginning to notice an improvement in his fitness, and in his new-found enthusiasm he decided to increase his training load by introducing a midweek sustained tempo run, first over six miles, and then the following week up to nine miles. In the last week of January he managed to run a total of 48 miles, his highest weekly mileage ever. If he continued at this rate, he figured, in a month's time he might be able to run a 60-mile week. Off that sort of training he might even be capable of running a 3½-hour marathon.

The only problem was that he was already starting to feel a little twinge in his left calf, a problem that seemed to get worse the longer and faster he ran. By now Stuart was running every evening of the week, in addition to a speed session on Saturday and his Sunday morning long run. He had little time left over to spend with his wife and baby daughter, or his non-running friends, let alone to see a doctor about his injury despite it getting sorer as the weeks went by. Finally, after a painful 15-mile run one Sunday in the middle of February – which reduced him at the end to little more than a hobble – he decided to take a few days' rest and get his injury seen by a specialist. His physiotherapist advised him to take three weeks off running.

'Hasten slowly'

Stuart's story is not uncommon among aspiring London Marathon runners, especially those attempting the event for the first time. He had plenty of determination to do the necessary training. He was willing to make sacrifices to fit more hours of running into his lifestyle. He even knew the right components of marathon training. His fault lay rather in his haste to build up his fitness too quickly, since he failed to realise that he had plenty of time on his side. Stuart would have done better had he adopted a more graduated approach to his training. Gains in fitness on a week-by-week basis might have then appeared smaller, but he would have reduced the risk of injury and given himself more chance of success over the extended period of a full three-month marathon build-up.

Q&A HOW IMPORTANT IS GOAL SETTING?

Appropriate goal setting for the marathon speaks volumes of your ability to make an accurate assessment of your capabilities and can therefore be a very helpful part of your marathon preparation. In general, modest goals often prove more effective than ambitious ones – as borne out by my own first marathon experience in 1993.

HARD AND EASY TRAINING

Stuart's story illustrates the importance of building up fitness gradually, as well as allowing sufficient time to recover from hard efforts in training. One way of achieving this is to plan some 'easy' days (or even an easier week) of running into the cycle of your training – before your body forces you to do so. This also has the benefit of allowing you to fit your running around other commitments in your life. For instance, if you are able to anticipate a particularly busy week ahead at work, or a family weekend away that will prevent you from doing your usual training, use this period to reduce your training and give your body a chance to recover.

The duration of such easy periods depends on the length and intensity of the previous period of training. In general, the harder and longer you train, the greater the need for recovery. In order to minimise the risks of breakdown you should limit the duration of your heaviest period of training to between two and three weeks. At lower volumes and intensities of training, there is

VIEW FROM THE ROAD
Geoff Wells: Building up the training

Geoff Wells learns the importance of long runs

In 2007 a colleague at work challenged me to run a half-marathon in under 2 hours. I was 43 and needed a challenge, and after a few months' training I ran 2:02:54. That made me get serious about my training. I started recording my training properly and entered a number of 10km races. By the end of 2009 I had covered 754 miles in the year and my half-marathon time was down to 1:48. This spurred me on to enter a marathon and in May 2010 I ran 4:16:54 in Edinburgh. Then through my club I got an entry to the 2011 London Marathon. In 2010 my yearly mileage was up to 1321 miles. Towards the end of 2010 I started an 18-week build-up to London, aiming for a sub-four hour time off a weekly programme of four or five training runs plus an occasional session in the gym. I was running between 35 and 50 miles per week. Each week I ran a hill/interval/fartlek session, a mid-paced run, two recovery runs and a long slow run at the weekend. My monthly mileage increased from 133 in December to 164 in January, then dropped to 134 for February and 149 for March. The drop in mileage in February was because I raced twice for my club in this month in place of my long run. In March I ran a 20-mile race in 2:58 and a half-marathon in 1:47. On average I was doing my long slow runs at around 9:40 minutes/mile. When I finished London in a time of 4:14, I felt that I was short of a couple of long runs, perhaps at a slightly faster pace. If there was one lesson I had learned, it was not to cut corners with my long runs.

EXPERT COMMENT
Bruce Tulloh: Structuring your marathon training

Bruce Tulloh, Richard's former coach, is one of Britain's best-known distance-running coaches

The first thing to decide is how much time you can give to your training and how much training your body will take. It takes less time to build up to 80km a week than to 160km. It also depends on your starting point. For a beginner, it might take six months to get up to 50km, and another three to four months of marathon training to get up to 80km. But in your second year of running, from a base of 40–50km per week, you could build up to 90–100km.

In your training programme you need to:

- build endurance through the weekly long runs and weekly total distance
- increase aerobic fitness through training at higher speeds
- develop all-round body strength.

In the context of the marathon, 'speedwork' means running at faster than marathon pace. So, for instance, once a week you should train at 5km or 10km pace, and once a week at half-marathon pace. A typical 10km-pace session might be 6 x 1km, with two to three minutes' rest in between, while a typical half-marathon-pace session might be 15 minutes running out, followed by a three-minute jog/walk, and 15 minutes running back.

In and among your efforts to train hard, you need to plan rest days or easy days, especially after long or hard runs. The body needs time to rebuild muscle glycogen, and also time for the strengthening of muscle. Most runners use a hard/easy/hard/easy pattern, plus one rest day, or a three-day hard/easy/rest pattern. You should allow one easy week out of every four, ideally before you run a race.

So how should you plan it all out? Work backwards from your race date and fix the dates of your long runs first and your races next. Then give yourself some short-term goals every three or four weeks to measure progress. You might try to run the same distance faster, or cover a longer distance. And then give yourself a reward every time you achieve a goal. When you make your overall plan, remember that the tapering in the last two weeks is the most important part – otherwise you won't get the value of the work that has gone before.

less need for easy periods of training, and it makes more sense to progress consistently over an extended period.

Whatever approach you take, you will undoubtedly benefit from having a plan and structure to your training. Use the training programmes on pp. 10–18 and pp. 204–213 as a guide for setting a schedule that suits your habits and your routine. 'If you fail to plan, you plan to fail', goes the saying – so make sure you have a plan before you get stuck into the training.

KEY POINTS

- Plan out a structure for your marathon build-up
- Assess your state of readiness at the start of your build-up, and adjust your goals accordingly
- Increase your training loads by small, gradual increments
- Divide your build-up into phases of progressively increased effort, with the hardest effort coming in the second half of the programme
- Stay on top of your training by scheduling easy days to follow particularly hard periods of training.

USEFUL TIPS
Coaching lessons

Sometimes, even good mountain climbers can benefit from the services of a guide. In this respect runners are no different – they too can often be helped through the advice of a coach, partner or friend. A good coach or adviser can act as the 'outside voice', understanding the desires and motivation of the athlete while still being detached from the physical and emotional stress of training. They are therefore better able to make more rational judgements when it comes to deciding on training. Coaching involves not merely the task of setting good training schedules; it also requires understanding of the athlete's particular needs.

Some of the important roles performed by the coach or adviser are:

- *Preventing you from becoming a slave to your training schedule.* As your individual circumstances change, it's important to be flexible with your training programme. Sometimes you may need to modify your training to make allowances for stresses in other areas of your life, or if you pick up a slight illness or injury. It's not always easy for the athlete alone to strike a balance between being disciplined about following a schedule and sensible about making such adjustments. A coach might be the person to help you.

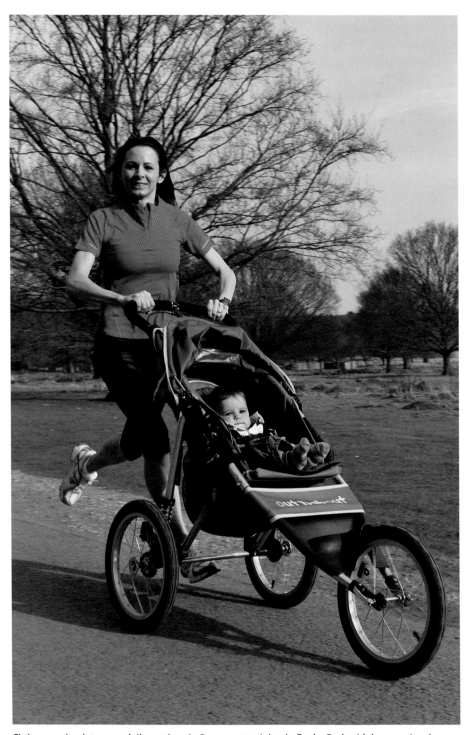

Fitting running into your daily routine: Jo Pavey out training in Bushy Park with her son Jacob

- *Telling you when you've done enough.* The competitive nature of the athlete often means that he or she may want to do more training, when more will result only in an increased risk of injury or illness. A coach can help reassure you that enough good training has been done and that you will benefit more from stopping now, before you get too tired.
- *Offering encouragement when you're feeling down.* In the course of any training programme, there are bound to be times when things don't work out quite as you had planned. Maybe you pick up a small injury and have to take a few days off running; maybe you feel too exhausted to train, or simply lose motivation for a while. At such times, it's often good to be able to turn to someone who is able and willing to support you in your training. Maybe they can join you for a bike ride when you are forced to take a break from running; or share some of the stress from another area of your life; or simply cook you a good meal to perk you up again.
- *Giving you confidence.* While fitness is usually measured in terms of your ability to cover set distances in certain times, your readiness to perform well either in training or competition also depends on how confident you are about accomplishing the task ahead of you. A coach can help in this respect, by being both supportive *and* realistic.

Every runner's requirements are different. Some will be better at thinking for themselves and at applying the brakes on training when they become too tired. Others might respond well to having a friend watch them train or follow them in the car or on the bike. Others will never be short of motivation but need reassurance that their training is going to plan. At some stage in the course of training, most of us benefit from the support and advice of a good friend. Remember too that the best coach for you isn't necessarily the person with the most running expertise; it may be the person who knows you best and understands what you are trying to get out of your running.

Here's a brief account of how my coach Bruce played a crucial part in helping me get the most out of my running.

Long before we first met, I knew of Bruce's reputation as both a highly accomplished athlete and coach. As one of Britain's best distance runners in the 1960s, and known for his barefoot running, Bruce is perhaps best remembered for winning the 1962 European 5000 metres in Belgrade. After he retired from international competition, he set a world record in 1969 by running from Los Angeles to New York in 64 days. Since then, as well as writing numerous books on training, he has helped many athletes achieve success at school, national and international level.

At the time of our first meeting in 1986, towards the end of my student days at Oxford, Bruce was coaching – in addition to his three children – a close friend and rival of mine from the Cambridge University team. This was my first regular contact with an athletics coach. From the outset Bruce started to give me advice about specific training sessions. He also taught me the importance of thinking beyond the next race. Over the many years that followed we enjoyed discussing my training and racing programme as I built up towards key races.

In the summer of 1989 I decided – with Bruce's encouragement – to take up a part-time teaching job at Marlborough College, rather than pursue the career path towards which my university education had been leading. I had just won my first international vest at the 1989 World Cross-Country Championships and was growing increasingly excited about my running. Due in no small part to Bruce's enthusiasm for my running, I was quickly able to make running more of a priority in my life.

Moving to Marlborough, where Bruce was also a schoolteacher, gave me the added advantage of being able to train under Bruce's close supervision. Some of my happiest memories go back to running over the Marlborough Downs in the early morning, after which I would end up at Bruce's house to do some stretching, before rushing back to my flat to shower in time for the start of morning lessons. In the afternoon I would join Bruce and Sue for a second workout either on the college fields or in the nearby woods. As we shared many hours of training together, they helped instil in me the confidence that I could compete at the highest level.

Sue and Bruce Tulloh, the two most important people in my running career

TRAINING FOR THE WORLD CUP
SAN SEBASTIAN, OCTOBER 1993

After a short break following my first marathon in Hamburg (see pp. 23–27), I had just under five months to prepare for my next one – representing Britain at the World Cup Marathon in October 1993*. This was too long a time to concentrate on one race, so I decided to spend the first two months trying to improve my performances on the track. This would leave 11 weeks for me to prepare for the marathon.

TRACK RACING IN THE SUMMER

I had recovered well from the marathon in Hamburg, and two weeks after the race I resumed my normal routine of training. My two months of track competition that summer centred on two races. The first one, coming just seven weeks after my marathon in Hamburg, turned out to be a huge success. Taking advantage of the good base of endurance from all my marathon training and a few good track workouts after the Hamburg event, I ran a personal best time of 27:40 in the Bislett Games 10,000m. For my second big race of the summer I decided to experiment with the idea of racing at sea-level on the same day as leaving altitude, in the hope of producing an equally good result in the Zurich 5000m at the Weltklasse meeting in early August. But to no avail. After a good spell of preparation in a training camp in St Moritz, I ran a disappointing 13:37, finishing well down the field. After Zurich I finished off my short track season with a 3000m race in the south of Germany, had a short holiday with friends on Lake Constance, and then returned home to start my build-up for the World Cup Marathon.

GETTING FOCUSED

I now had 11 weeks to prepare for the race. It was time to get serious again about the marathon. Having spent much of the summer 'thinking track', the aim now was to 'think distance'. Since my first marathon had been run off an eight-week build-up (following a viral problem earlier in the year), for

---

*From 1985 to 1995, the IAAF World Cup Marathon took place every two years, as a separate event from the IAAF World Championships which encompassed the whole range of track and field disciplines. In addition to the individual race, the event involved a team competition; this was decided by the lowest aggregate finishing times of the first three runners from each country.

ALTITUDE TRAINING

The timing of an athlete's descent from altitude can be crucial to success. Theories abound about the optimum time for competition at sea-level after completing a spell of training at altitude. For instance, many Kenyan runners who live at altitude prefer to race immediately after their descent – otherwise, as I once heard a Kenyan coach explaining, 'it's like gradually losing the fizz from an opened can of beer'. By contrast, the majority of European runners, myself included, have found that the best results come in the 10–20 day period after returning to sea level.

this marathon I felt I had time on my side so I deliberately held back in the intensity of my training for the first five weeks. There was no need to apply maximum effort from the start of the build-up; the really hard phase of the training would commence six weeks before the race.

With Bruce's help I planned two phases of hard training to prepare for the marathon. The first phase lasted five weeks and was done at sea level. It was made up of consistently good weekly mileage for four weeks, followed by an easy week leading up to a half-marathon race. Then came the second and hardest phase of the training, where I spent three weeks at altitude. An easy week back home followed, leading up to a 10-mile race. By then the hard training was over and I was already starting to ease down for the marathon (see Table 2.4).

Over the course of the build-up, I aimed first to increase the distance of the long run – for which pace was less important than duration. Then, having completed an 'overdistance' run of 30 miles, I switched my attention to improving the speed of these longer runs. By the end of the second phase of hard training I was running my long runs at close to race-pace effort. Table 2.5 illustrates how the speed, and therefore the toughness, of these runs increased as the race approached.

NO HOLDING BACK

My final phase of hard training started the day after the Great North Run on Tyneside, where I had finished third in a time of 1:01:53. I flew out to the Pyrenees for three weeks' training at altitude, during which time I ran over 390 miles in 21 days. This represented an increase in volume of 10 per cent on the training I had done in the first half of the build-up. (For a comparison of my weekly schedule in these two phases of the build-up, see Table 2.6.)

Training at my hardest at this phase of the build-up, from six weeks to three weeks before the race, meant that my confidence was high as I approached

TABLE 2.4 BUILDING UP TO THE WORLD CUP MARATHON

Week	Relative intensity of training	Hard sessions	Total training
1	Moderate	Hill workout, 4 × 3km road	184km
2	Hard	38km long run, 2 × (8 × 600m) grass, fartlek	188km
3	Hard	48km long run, 15km tempo run, hill workout	190km
4	Moderate	4 × 4km road, 6 × 1 km dirt road, 8 × 400m	172km
5	Easy	39km long run	104km
6	Moderate	Half-marathon race, 40km long run	194km
7	Very hard	4 × 3km grass, fartlek, 16km tempo run	240km
8	Very hard	10 × 1km grass/ track, 40km long run	192km
9	Easy	8km tempo run, 16 × 200m strides	160km

Two weeks to go to marathon: 10-mile race followed by reduction in training

TABLE 2.5 INCREASING THE PACE OF THE LONG RUN

Weeks before marathon	Length of run	Time (hrs:mins)	Pace (mins/km)
11 weeks	30km	2:00	4:00
10 weeks	38km	2:32	4:00
8½ weeks	48km	3:07	3:55
7 weeks	39km	2:22	3:40
5 weeks	40km	2:23	3.35
3 weeks	40km	2:15	3:22

TABLE 2.6 COMPARISON OF WEEKLY TRAINING CYCLES IN THE BUILD-UP

7-day training cycle – 1st half of build-up			7-day training cycle – 2nd half of build-up		
DAY		SESSION	DAY		SESSION
1	a.m.	10km steady	1	7.00a.m.	7km easy
	p.m.	4 × 3km road, 3 min recovery		10.00a.m.	16km tempo run
				p.m.	8km easy
2	a.m.	10km easy	2	a.m.	18km easy
	p.m.	6km easy			
3	a.m.	38km long run (2hrs 32min)	3	7.00a.m.	7km easy
				10.00a.m.	16km steady +
				p.m.	6 × 200m strides
					8km easy
4	a.m.	9km easy	4	7.00a.m.	7km easy
	p.m.	13km steady + 6 × 100m strides		10.00a.m.	10 × 1km grass/ track, 3min recovery
				p.m.	
					10km easy
5	a.m.	10km steady	5	7.00a.m.	8km easy
	p.m.	18km steady		10.00a.m.	17km steady +
					8 × 100m strides
6	a.m.	10km steady	6	a.m.	16km steady
	p.m.	2 × (8 × 600m) grass, 1 min/5 min recovery		p.m.	8km steady
7	a.m.	17km easy	7	a.m.	40km long run (2hrs 15min)
	p.m.	11km steady			
		Total 110 miles			**Total 125 miles**

the final stages of my preparation. But it also meant that I had time to recover from these exertions, and be fully rested for when the race came.

READY TO RACE

'Do the Chinese really drink turtle blood or not?' This was the question on the lips of every athletics journalist as the teams arrived in San Sebastian on the eve of the race. Six weeks previously, at their National Championships in Beijing, Chinese female distance runners had rewritten the record books for the 1500m, 3000m and 10,000m events. Now they had announced their intention of coming to race in the World Cup Marathon. Would another world best be created at this distance?

To the dismay of attending journalists and television crews, the Chinese women helped themselves to a large plate of pasta – just like everyone else.

My race plan was to stay with the leaders until the closing stages, at which point I would make a decisive move. I would cover any attempts by my opponents to break clear in the first 20 miles of the race by increasing my pace, but without accelerating too fast. Unless the pace was very slow, the key to conserving energy for the race's final stages lay in even-paced running.

The race threw up little in the way of surprises. A leading pack of about 20 runners reached the halfway point in 1:04:52. Soon after passing halfway, the home favourite Diego Garcia increased the tempo in an attempt to break clear. But the chasing group covered his move, as they did a few kilometres later when the leading Kenyan in the race adopted a similar tactic.

From 30km to 38km I watched and waited. As we approached a slight uphill

DIETARY SUPPLEMENTS

Dietary supplements are commonly used by elite athletes to enhance performance, as well as to diminish the risks associated with hard training and fatigue. Today, more than ever before, exceptional athletic performance is likely to arouse suspicions as to the legality of any such aids. In the late 1990s, following revelations at the 1998 Tour de France indicating the likelihood of widespread drug abuse, there was much speculation in distance-running circles over the extent of use of the banned drug erythropoietin (EPO), which boosts the body's oxygen-carrying capacity.) On the eve of the World Cup race in 1993 there was, not surprisingly, considerable interest in what the Chinese athletes may or may not have been using. For more information on ergogenic aids, see Chapter 4, p. 82.

(leading into a tunnel under the hillside which brought us back into the town centre), I made a decisive move. Within the space of 500m I had opened up a 10-second lead. From then on, it was a matter of hanging on until the finish – which I just managed to do, winning the race by a slender eight-second margin. I had made it hard for myself by injecting such a dramatic change of pace, but in the end it had paid off. My winning time was 2:10:03, though I felt I could have run faster still had the race been run differently. For now, victory and a championship title – Britain's first in the marathon for 19 years – was all that mattered.

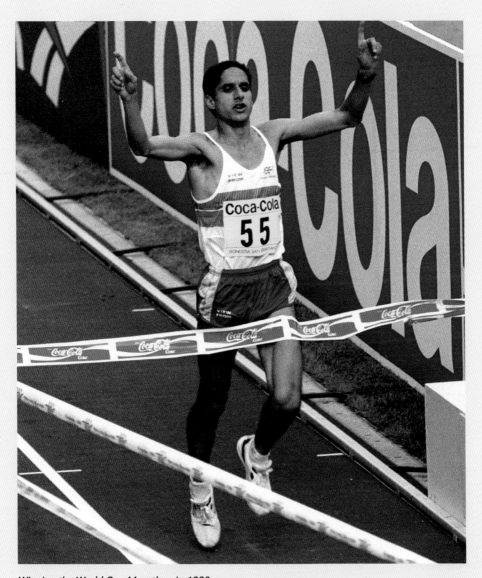

Winning the World Cup Marathon in 1993

03

The women's marathon world record holder Paula Radcliffe toughs it out en route to a third place finish in the 2011 Berlin Marathon

RACE-SPECIFIC TRAINING

BUILDING ENDURANCE AND SPEED

The end product of any marathon-training plan should be good endurance. What is meant by the term 'endurance', and how do you go about acquiring it?

BUILDING ENDURANCE

From the point of view of the marathon runner, you could think of endurance as the ability to cope with unreasonable levels of tiredness for an uncomfortably long period of time. In terms of the process of developing endurance, however, this need not be quite as painful as the description above implies. Time is on your side: remember the rule of building up gradually. Having a structure to your training is also important, since this will help you monitor your progress and grow in confidence as your fitness improves. Good training also involves striking the right balance between long, slow running and faster-paced efforts.

> **'You could think of endurance as the ability to cope with unreasonable levels of tiredness for an uncomfortably long period of time.'**

Quality versus quantity

Many runners who decide to run a marathon are motivated by the thought of completing the course within a set time – for instance, improving on their previous best time or breaking the three-, four- or five-hour barrier for the distance. Setting yourself these kinds of time goals means that you have to pay attention to the endurance aspect of your preparation – the ability simply to keep going – as well as to the speed at which you train.

The purpose of your weekly long run, together with maintaining a good overall volume of miles run each week, is to develop endurance. Beyond a certain amount of long, slow running, however, your fitness will further improve only if you introduce some faster-paced running into your training programme. In the context of training for a marathon, these 'speed' sessions have little to do with flat-out sprinting. Some are designed to improve your 10km running speed, while others are intended to improve your efficiency at running at your marathon pace. In other words, they are tailored towards preparing you specifically for certain races. As a mid-term goal for the first half of your marathon build-up, you should be aiming to run a half-marathon. To this end, the best training pace for your sessions of faster running is your 10km race pace. In the second half of your build-up, however, the emphasis should switch towards running closer to your marathon race pace. (This is discussed in more detail on pp. 54–55.)

There will always be a trade-off between quality and quantity. A higher overall weekly mileage, or a longer endurance run, will leave you with less energy to run well in your faster-paced workouts. This chapter should help you understand how best to achieve this balance between fast and slow running.

Q&A: HOW IMPORTANT IS MY RUNNING STYLE?

There are plenty of examples of world-class performers who do not possess the perfect effortless running action. Besides, running style is one of those things that is very hard to change. This is not to say, however, that you should not consider how you can optimise your own way of running. Even slight changes to how you hold your shoulders or carry your arms can influence how you feel in a competition and thus your overall performance. At the very least it may be useful to watch yourself run by getting somebody film you running on a treadmill to see if you can make any energy-saving adjustments to your running action.

Establishing a weekly training routine

Developing fitness involves a continual cycle of stress and recovery. First you subject yourself to a certain level of stress, and then you allow yourself time to recover before progressing to a greater level of stress – all within the limits of your individual capability. You can think of this process as occurring both on a day-to-day basis and over a longer period – hence the importance of phases of hard and easy training described on p. 35. In terms of structuring a weekly training routine, you should intersperse days of moderate or hard effort with days of either light training or rest.

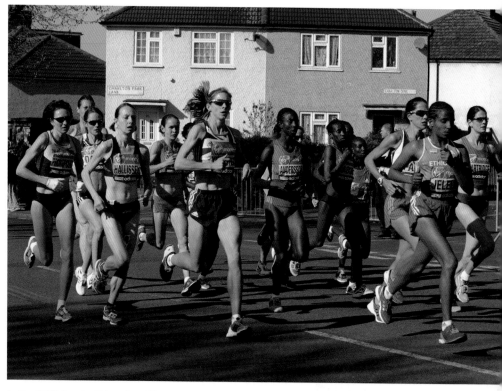

In the 2012 London Marathon Claire Hallisey (second from left) ran a PB of 2:27:44 and won a place on the British team for the 2012 London Olympics

Starting with your weekly long run (which for most people takes place at the weekend), you should aim to do two more hard sessions in the course of a week's training. Whereas the effort involved in the long run comes from its duration, in the other two hard efforts it comes from faster-paced running. Depending on your level of fitness, the rhythm of your training week might look like the week shown in Table 3.1.

Your Thursday and Saturday sessions can be interchangeable – people in work might find that they have more time and energy for a harder session on

TABLE 3.1 TYPICAL RHYTHM OF A TRAINING WEEK

SUN	MON	TUES	WED	THUR	FRI	SAT
Long run	Easy or rest	Hard effort	Easy	Hard effort	Easy or rest	Steady

Saturday. On the other hand, to ensure that you are fresh and well-rested for a big effort in your long run on Sunday, you might prefer to do your second hard session earlier in the week. Use a programme that fits in best around your lifestyle, enabling you to perform well in your hard efforts as well as to recover well afterwards.

Let's now look in more detail at the nature of your harder sessions.

The long run: 'time on your feet'

The single most important component of your training programme is the weekly long run. Over the course of a marathon build-up, you should aim to increase the duration of this run so that towards the end of your build-up you are running for a good proportion of the time it will take you to complete the marathon itself. I say 'duration' rather than 'distance', because the speed of these runs is less important than how long they are. So, at least in the early stages of the build-up, you might prefer to quantify these long runs in terms of 'time on your feet' rather than as a certain distance.

In the early stages of the build-up to my first marathon, I was struggling to carry out my normal load of training without becoming excessively tired. In place of my usual long run of 18–20 miles (which I would normally run in under two hours), my coach therefore suggested that I went out for some 'long jogs' (walking interspersed with light running) of up to three hours' duration. In these training efforts I would cover around 25 miles – admittedly, at a lower level of effort than for my usual long run. Still, these long slow runs gave me a training benefit. They also helped me get used to the thought of just how far 26 miles actually was, coming from a racing background where six miles was considered to be part of 'long-distance running'.

How long and how far?

The length or duration of your long run will depend on:

- your current level of fitness – beginners, for example, who have followed the training outlined in Chapter 1, should aim to walk/run for at least an hour at the start of their build-up, and increase this to three hours as they approach the race
- the time and energy available to you
- the stage you are at in your build-up
- your expected finishing time in the marathon.

Obviously, the fitter you are, the further you should be able to run. On the other hand, if you expect to take five hours to complete your marathon, it makes sense to do at least one long effort during the course of your build-up of three hours minimum.

Broadly speaking, your long weekly effort should last between two and three hours. If you try to run for longer than three hours on a regular basis, you run the risk of exhaustion. (More advanced runners may decide to do one of their long training runs over a course of more than 26 miles. But I recommend this only for those who can cover this distance in training in not much more than three hours. The benefit of this kind of run is as much psychological as physical.)

Once you have reached the point where you are confident of keeping going for two hours or more, you might then want to think about how far you are running. Beginners should attempt at least one run of 18–20 miles before the marathon; more advanced runners should aim to do four or five runs of 20 miles or more. (My coach devised the following guide: if the total distance

VIEW FROM THE ROAD
John Britton: How I trained for the marathon

John Britton did what he previously never thought possible
I never thought that I would run a marathon, as after each of the half marathons I'd run I felt so exhausted over the last two miles that starting again was just inconceivable. A friend told me that the same thing happens at all longer distances – it doesn't matter how far you set out to run, it's the last two miles that hurt.

The most important part of my training was the long runs. During a five-month preparation period, I did two long runs each month over distances from 15 to 21 miles. Then, three weeks before the marathon, I did one run of 24 miles. I did all of these runs at my steady speed; I tried to do faster periods but it never seemed to work. I built up to running about 40–50 miles a week in the month before the race and have never felt fitter or better. As my marathon was in September, I did almost all of my training in the early morning sun along and around the River Trent. It felt fantastic.

On race day I was nervous, but in my head I was sure I would finish because I only had two more miles to do! It turned out that miles 14 to 20 were the difficult ones, mentally more than physically, but from around 20 miles to the finish the exhilaration just built up, despite the physical exhaustion. I finished in a time of 4 hours and 50 minutes. It was one of the best feelings of my life.

of your five longest runs over the course of your build-up to a marathon amounts to 100 miles or more, you should feel well prepared for the event.) How this distance is gradually increased over the course of a build-up is illustrated in Table 2.3 on p. 34.

Your longest runs, just like your heaviest weeks of training, should come in the third quarter of your build-up – between six and three weeks before your marathon. To reduce the risk of injury, resist the temptation of attempting very long runs too early in the build-up, unless they are in the form of long 'hikes'. You should also leave sufficient time between your last long training run and the marathon itself, to ensure that you have fully recovered from the exertions of training. This means that your last really long run (18 miles or more) should be done three weeks before your marathon. (If you have missed a considerable amount of training earlier in the build-up, you might resort to doing this run at the latest two weeks before the marathon.)

Introducing some faster-paced running

In the early stages of your build-up, the focus of these sessions should be simply to run at a quicker tempo than your normal 'steady' running pace, over relatively short distances. (For a definition of 'steady' running, *see* Chapter 1, p. 9.) Sessions of short, faster running will add variety to your weekly routine

VIEW FROM THE ROAD
Nigel Sarjudeen: The challenge of training

Nigel Sarjudeen on training and race preparations for the marathon
For many years I would have classified myself as an occasional runner. Then in 2006 when I turned 44, I suffered a mild heart attack and, as part of my cardiac rehabilitation programme, I started doing organised fitness sessions. Within a year I ran the annual Brighton half-marathon, something I have done every year since. In 2009 when the first Brighton Marathon was announced, I thought this was too good an opportunity to miss and got my place. The biggest challenge of training for the marathon was fitting in the weekly long run during the three months leading up to the race. A year later I was back training for my second Brighton Marathon and found that a good way to do my long run was to fit it in around the weekly 5km 'park run' in Hove Park. Also, the timing of the half-marathon, just two months before the full one, was an ideal stepping stone midway through my marathon preparation.

of training. Instead of lapsing into a plod every time you go out to train, you will be able to focus on making sustained efforts during the course of a given workout, punctuated with short periods of recovery. These sessions play as important a role in raising your level of fitness as will an increase in your overall volume of training.

Most runners tend to get more out of a varied training programme – where the variety comes from doing your training runs at different speeds and with different degrees of effort. Your marathon training will therefore include the following sessions of faster-paced running.

- A 'repetition' session (e.g. 4 × 5 min with 3 min recovery) – this involves making a hard effort for five minutes of fast running, followed by a recovery of three minutes of slow jogging (or walking). This cycle is repeated three more times. How fast you run in each individual section (or 'interval') of the workout depends on the overall length of the session. Since you should aim to run each repetition at roughly the same speed, it is important that you spread your effort over the entire workout. As you get tired towards the end of the session you might have to make more of an effort to maintain the same running pace as at the start.
- A simpler variation of combined fast and slow running is a 'fartlek' (literally meaning 'speed-play') session. Here, you alternate fast and slow running – either according to feeling (a *spontaneous fartlek*) or, as many runners prefer, with reference to time or distance (a *structured fartlek*, e.g. 1 min fast/1 min easy, or 6 lampposts fast/4 easy).
- A 'pace run' or 'tempo run', which involves a longer, sustained effort of brisk running without reaching maximum speed. Ideally, this should be run over a set distance – perhaps on a quiet stretch of road that you have measured beforehand by car or bike. In these sessions you will practise the art of maintaining a strong running pace over a longer period. From them you should also develop a sense of pace judgement which will prove useful when it comes to running your marathon.
- A session of fast strides (e.g. 6–8 × 150m), at the end of a steady run. Here you are running close to your maximum speed without actually sprinting.

More information on building speed into your training is given on p. 57 of this chapter – *Race pace*.

Monitor and modify

As your training progresses, increased fitness levels might leave you feeling that you need less recovery time between each hard session. Remember, however, that your hard workouts will actually become more demanding as you get closer to your marathon. You will also be running more miles each

VIEW FROM THE ROAD
Adrian Marriott: How I trained for the marathon

Adrian Marriott surprises himself with a time of 2:22:14 in his debut marathon

Heading into my first marathon in Amsterdam I was confident that I could last the distance. I was coming from a cross-country background where I regularly ran up to 20 miles for my long Sunday run. But I had never raced further than 12km. Having seen many experienced runners have a terrible last few miles in their first marathon, I wanted to train in such a way that made it less likely for this to happen to me. My key training session was the long tempo run of up to 25km, which I tried to run at my target race pace, or at least at my race pace effort. These runs got me used to maintaining my pace when tired. I did six of these runs during a 12-week build-up, as well as shorter tempo runs at half-marathon speed. I also ran a couple of miles at race pace in the latter stages of my long runs, just to get used to running at speed when really tired. This preparation, and constantly telling myself to hold back in the first half of the marathon, actually helped me to run faster over the second half of the race distance, which also meant that I passed lots of runners who were slowing down. The result: a strong finish and a positive experience for my first marathon.

week and covering more miles on your weekly long run. So resist the urge to do much more than your programme for the week allows. On the other hand, you may find that you are struggling to cope with the overall intensity of your training. If this is the case, it is probably better to reduce the number of hard efforts each week rather than run them at a lower level of effort. You can modify your training programme in the following ways:

- in place of a hard session, run a 'half-session' of a steady run plus strides
- if you're not yet recovered in time for your next hard session, give yourself another day
- remember that sometimes you may derive more benefit from having a complete day off running than from going out for a slow plod.

Your performance in the marathon is the product of weeks of good training, so one fewer hard session will hardly make a difference. It is better to be consistent with your training and feel good about it, than let it get the better of you. So learn to be flexible with your training programme and adapt it to suit your individual requirements.

RACE PACE – BUILDING SPEED

As you get nearer to your marathon, you should have a growing sense that your reserves of endurance are being brought to their peak. You should derive confidence from knowing that you are able to handle greater volumes of training than at the start of your build-up, and that you have gradually increased the length of your weekly long run.

What about the progression of your sessions of faster running? In your sessions of repetition and tempo running you should be thinking about running further rather than faster: you should aim to develop your ability to maintain a good running pace over increasingly longer distances.

Remember that training should be specific to the event. As you begin to concentrate your thoughts on running your marathon, during the second half of your build-up, you will benefit by doing some of your training runs at a pace that more closely approximates your intended running speed in the marathon itself.

The sessions described below – in the form of 'repetitions' run over shorter intervals, and 'tempo runs' over slightly longer distances – show the kind of progression that your training should follow over the course of a build-up.

Repetitions and tempo runs
Repetitions
- *First-time marathoners*: three months before your marathon you might be able to run 4×1km (or 4×5 minutes), with three minutes recovery, at your 10km pace. Six weeks later you should be fit enough to attempt 3×8–10 minutes, with three minutes recovery, at around half-marathon pace.
- *Advanced runners*: progressing from 3×3km, with three minutes recovery, at your 10-mile race pace to 2×5–6km, with four minutes recovery, at your marathon pace.

In other words, as your training progresses, the emphasis shifts towards running fast over longer intervals. Short recovery periods more closely approximate the feeling of the sustained effort required in running a marathon, so it is better to reduce the recovery time rather than increase the running speed of the faster sections.

Tempo runs (or pace runs)
- *First-time marathoners*: three months before your marathon you might attempt a tempo run of three miles at slightly slower than 10km race pace.

EXPERT COMMENT
Laura Kirk: Gait analysis

Laura Kirk is a running shoe specialist

There is a common perception that gait analysis is all about getting somebody to run on a treadmill, watching how their foot lands and then observing through slow-motion replay analysis how far an individual's footfall deviates from a perpendicular straight line.

My approach is quite different. For me, gait analysis involves a more holistic examination of the runner so that I can give the best possible advice about footwear for any individual. By 'holistic' I mean considering their running pace, foot shape and general anatomical features, as well as looking at how many years they have been running and any previous injuries. Gait analysis is important because it can go a long way towards preventing injury and also helps athletes to run more efficiently. Often the best results come by working hand in hand with advice passed on from sports physiotherapists treating the same patients.

My first step in conducting a gait analysis is to find out about the athlete's running history, including their goals and aspirations, and to understand what type of a runner they are. As part of my initial prescription I also look at their feet and lower limbs and try to determine whether they need to be referred to a sports physiotherapist or podiatrist.

Next I try to determine what I call the 'fit window' in terms of the most appropriate shoe for the runner, along a wide spectrum from soft/flexible shoes to hard/'motion control' designs. I offer a number of options to my customers, knowing that the choice between brands is often a personal matter. I like runners to try on the shoes, walk round the store and then run in them, preferably outside.

The treadmill part of my analysis is really just the finishing touch. As I watch the athlete running on the treadmill, I observe how the foot lands and whether the shoe is protecting the foot adequatly as it rolls inward upon impact with the ground. I also try to make other observations, for example whether the hip is extending well. There might be other clues: what sound is the shoe making upon impact – is it 'slapping down' or is it quiet? These are subtle things, but they can be more easily spotted by somebody watching from the outside, and I see this as part of my job.

My job is to sell shoes to customers, but doing my job well is just as much about sending runners away happy, knowing that they have bought the shoes that are best for their running.

Six weeks later you might be ready to do a tempo run of between five and six miles at just below half-marathon pace.

- *Advanced runners*: three months before, a tempo run of 4–5 miles; six weeks later a tempo run of 8–10 miles.

The pace of your tempo runs should be 'brisk, yet controlled'. Remind yourself of the purpose of the workout: to rehearse your race effort. With the exception of the elite, there is no need to attempt very long tempo runs.

Stay within your limits

Once you have done a few sessions of repetition and tempo running, you should start to get an idea of how fast you are running even without having to look at your watch. You should aim to run as relaxed and efficiently as possible, with a view to maintaining an even pace over an extended distance. The toughness of the session comes also from having to concentrate on making a more sustained effort.

Variations on a theme

The one drawback of the tempo run in training is that it is often difficult to maintain effort and concentration for an extended period – especially if you're

RUNNING ECONOMY

Take a look at the world's best marathon runners, and you will notice certain general features of their style of running. Their neck and shoulders remain relaxed even as their body grows tired. Their arms are held loosely near to their waist and use up minimal energy. Since they use a short, quick stride pattern, they have a relatively low knee lift. These features broadly constitute what is known as 'running economy' – a style of running that allows you to conserve energy over a long period. The more you are able to run with such efficiency, the greater will be your chances of success at the marathon. (Note too that physical efficiency is complemented by exercising mental restraint in running your marathon – see Useful Tips on planning a race strategy, pp. 103–105.)

Running efficiently up and down hills: when running downhill, try to lean slightly forwards and carry your arms low at your side, only using them if necessary to keep your balance. When running uphill, move more on to your toes, shorten your stride and use your arms in a brisk forward-and-back motion to sustain your speed.

running alone. If this is the case, you can achieve a similar training effect by breaking the distance into shorter segments with only short (1–2 min) recoveries. For example:

- *First-time marathoners*: a four-mile continuous run (around 35 mins) can be replaced with a session of 2 × 2 miles (around 16–18 mins) with a 2-minute recovery after the first effort
- *Advanced runners*: an eight-mile tempo run can be replaced with 3-mile-2-mile-3-mile with a 1–2 minute recovery.

As with the repetition sessions above, the short recoveries ensure that the whole workout feels like one continuous effort – although you have the benefit of being able to concentrate on one section at a time. For the elite runner, you can replace a short jog recovery with a segment of reduced-intensity running.

EXPERT COMMENT
Richard Nerurkar: Training for a marathon in a fitness gym

Are you someone who enjoys the feeling and motivation of training in the company of others in a more warm and friendly environment, or who is more at home with a routine of regular visits to your local fitness centre? If so, here are a few tips to guide your approach to marathon training:

First, let's look at the advantages:
- it is easier to stay motivated in the company of others
- your training is less dependent on the weather and daylight
- it may be safer and warmer, reducing the risk of illness/ injury
- there are more opportunities to vary your training
- it may offer the opportunity for recuperative activities (e.g. massage, sauna/steam).

And the disadvantages:
- ultimately there is no substitute for going out and simply running when training for the marathon
- running long distances on a treadmill can be boring
- running on the road feels different from running on a treadmill
- the maximum time allowed on treadmill may be limited depending on fitness centre.

A few pointers for your training in the gym:

- Organise your training according to time spent doing various activities: e.g. 20 minutes of exercise bike, 20 minutes of running, 10 minutes step, and 10 minutes machines + 10 minutes stretching. Over the course of your marathon build up, more time should be given to the running component of training.

- Use your sessions of treadmill running to get used to running at certain paces and to monitor improvements in fitness in terms of time taken to cover certain intervals/ distances. In general, treadmill sessions offer you the chance to regulate your pace more closely and give more priority to speed than to distance.

- Take advantage of non-running exercise in the gym (e.g. exercise bikes and step machines) for building fitness through 'low-impact' exercise, especially following training which results in soreness/stiffness in lower limbs.

Even if gym training forms the basis of your weekly training, try to ensure at least one long weekly run outdoors as one important component of your marathon training and to remind yourself of what is involved in the competition.

Conditioning work in the gym has been important for Haile Gebrselassie

Thus a 15km tempo run might be done as a continuous cycle of five efforts, each comprising 2km at marathon pace followed by 1km at 30 seconds slower than marathon pace.

The structure of your marathon training should enable you to improve your ability to run further at a given speed (rather than to run faster at a set distance – though as you get fitter, you will quite likely achieve both these goals). Feeling strong rather than speedy is the best way to develop a sense of readiness for competition.

Remember too, as your training progresses, to 'hasten slowly'. Try to stay on top of your training, and pace yourself through the various stages of your build-up. A sense of *timing* – in terms of bringing yourself to a peak of physical and mental readiness – is crucial for good performance.

KEY POINTS
- Pay attention both to the speed of your runs and the distance covered
- Intersperse harder sessions of training with days of rest or easy running
- Measure your long run by time, not by distance
- Extend your range of distance over the course of the build-up
- Practise running for a sustained effort at close to your marathon race pace
- Reduce the recovery intervals within sessions as you get closer to the race
- Try to bring yourself to a peak of fitness at the right time.

USEFUL TIPS
Race-specific training – devising training routes
Some of your main training efforts during your marathon build-up – for instance, running at a constant pace over an extended distance, or practising taking drinks during a long run – can be made easier if you give some thought to where you run these sessions. Here are a few useful considerations, followed by some information on how I have devised routes for key sessions performed during the build-up to some of my marathons:

- What is the nature of the terrain?
- Will you be affected by traffic?
- How can you measure the route?

EXPERT COMMENT
Alan Storey: Training for a marathon

Alan Storey, former Technical Director of endurance running at UK Athletics

First, let's think about long runs: these are vital in your preparation, both for the mind and the body. You should try to increase the length of these as the marathon approaches, with the longest run taking place three to six weeks before the event, as best fits in with your individual programme. First-timers might only manage 15–18 miles for their longest run, but many experienced marathoners will include runs of up to 30 miles, or even up to six hours if you are Japanese! Regular marathon runners will include long runs in their training throughout the year.

Now, let's think about **speedwork**: you need to do some of your running at a quicker pace than your marathon race pace so that you can feel relaxed when going at racing speed. More experienced runners include some form of speedwork in the form of repetitions or intervals either on the road, grass or track. It is less important for those just wishing to get around a marathon, or for those running one for the first time, who will be concentrating more on running regularly and staying clear of injury.

Which brings us to the topic of **rest days**: training only works if, after you impose a stress on the body, you allow it to recover and then adapt. No stress or no recovery means that there is no adaptation, and therefore no improvement. Even the very best runners such as Paula Radcliffe take regular rest days: they are very important both to allow the body to regenerate, and to give the mind a rest from the daily grind of training. In the easing-down period, as the marathon approaches, they are vital.

So, how can you reach a **peak of fitness**? It is often difficult to know when you are reaching a peak, in terms of the amount of training you can take. You may be feeling permanently tired, yet can still manage to do that day's training. If this happens close to the race, you should start to take it very easy; further away you should review your training and see whether a short rest will help before you return to full training. Your fitness peak will be achieved once you have given yourself time to adapt – perhaps about two weeks after the hard training is over. The danger is that you will be fit too early or very tired when you start the race. In terms of performance, you should expect to see your training and racing times improve as the marathon approaches, and you may need shorter recovery periods in between or after sessions of hard training.

- Is there any protection from the wind?
- How can I arrange to take drinks during my run?

Tips for devising routes
- *Practising a constant pace over an extended period* (e.g. 3 × 10 mins). It might help to seek out stretches of preferably flat and relatively traffic-free running. I have used a range of venues for this, including riverside towpaths, disused airfields and dirt roads through forests. On quiet but wide country roads I have also run sessions accompanied (at a distance of 10–20m behind) by someone on a bike or in a car, to alert other vehicles to my presence.
- *Repetitions over kilometres/miles.* Measure out your course beforehand by bike (if running on a traffic-free dirt road) or by car. Where possible choose a relatively sheltered area, which might allow you to run the course in both directions while keeping your times/effort constant.
- *Practising the art of holding yourself back.* Use a lap course (e.g. three laps of a 10km route for a long 30km run), and try to increase your speed over each consecutive lap – saving your biggest effort for the end of the session.
- *Taking drinks on the run* (remember that you want to drink once every half-hour during a 2½hr run). Here, you might have to rely on a coach or friend to accompany you on a bike or in a car. Alternatively, use a 'loop' course, which allows you to take a drink (set up beforehand) at the same point on each loop. Ideally, you might benefit from both options.

Using races to monitor your progress

By the time you start your marathon build-up, you should have some experience of what it's like to take part in a race – perhaps you've just completed a local fun run, or maybe you've even got your first half-marathon behind you.

Taking part in a race gives you a different kind of experience from simply going out for a training run. You learn to cope with pre-race nerves as you line up at the start with crowds of other runners. In the race itself it is important that you exercise good pace judgement, resisting for instance the temptation to start too quickly. Similarly, nothing in training can quite compare with that post-race feeling of satisfaction and relief from having completed the course.

As well as becoming more familiar with the race-specific experience, doing some races in the course of your build-up can further your preparation for the marathon in a number of ways.

- *Races represent useful short-term goals and serve to break up the slog of training.* For instance, you might aim to run a 10-mile race after one month of your build-up, and a half-marathon at the end of the second month.
- *A good race performance can give a boost to your training.* You start to

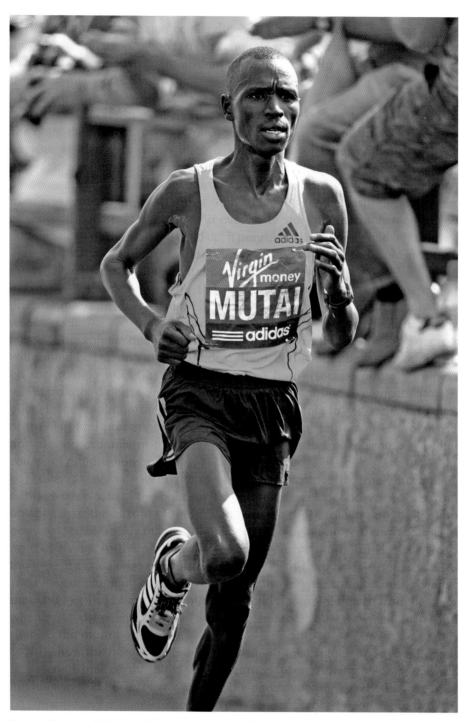

Kenya's Emmanuel Mutai on his way to winning the 2011 London Marathon in a new course record of 2:04:40

see the fruits of your training, and once you have recovered from your race you can resume your normal training with renewed vigour.

- *Races further develop your fitness.* Harder than any exertion you may make in training, racing places greater stress on your system, so you may need longer to recover than after a hard training session. You should not plan to race more than twice a month during your build-up, otherwise you will have too many interruptions to your normal training routine.

- *Races help you to 'rest'.* Being obsessive creatures, many runners are notoriously bad at allowing themselves an easy week of training. Races are one way of ensuring that you plan one or two periods of lighter training into your build-up. Remember that you are more likely to perform well in a race if you have rested well in the few days beforehand – a pattern you should follow even if you are treating the race as part of training towards a longer-term goal.

- *Races will help you determine a realistic target for your marathon race pace.* For instance, if you can run 10 miles in under 69 minutes, or a half-marathon in around 92 minutes (7:00 min/mile), then your target race pace for the marathon would be around 7:30–7:40 min/mile. My coach has a method for predicting the finishing time in the marathon, based on performances at the half-marathon. This involves doubling the half-marathon time and then adding 7.5 per cent. As an example, if your half-marathon time is 1:31:30, your goal for the marathon might be $(91.5 \times 2) + 7.5$ per cent = 3:16.

Below is an example of how I used a 10-mile race to monitor my progress as I built up towards the 1997 London Marathon.

Before starting my build-up to the 1997 London Marathon, I had done a couple of tough cross-country races on the continent. Thereafter I did only one more race, halfway through the really hard period of training and six weeks before the marathon itself. The event I chose was the Woking 10-mile race, a popular event for runners preparing for the London Marathon. Woking is conveniently situated only about a half-hour's drive from our home. The proximity of the race venue meant that I minimised the stress of travelling to and from the competition.

The race was usually won in a time of around 50 minutes. My training up to this point in my build-up indicated that I was capable of running between 46:30 and 47:00 minutes, so I was not expecting to meet much serious opposition. Nevertheless, I wanted to run hard, feel confident about the progress of my training, and ensure a good last race before the marathon. I therefore planned an easier week of training leading up to the event, reducing the volume of my training in race week by about a third and holding off from doing any really hard workouts.

VIEW FROM THE ROAD
Liz McColgan: How I trained for the marathon

Former world 10,000m champion and London Marathon winner, Liz McColgan, rolls back the years for another crack at London

There were two reasons why I decided to run in London in 2007. One was because I was a patron of Leukemia Research, the other was because my Dad had died of cancer just two months before the race. I know that he would have loved to see me run again there. The good thing I can now say is that I raised a lot of money for a great charity. Some years back, I was forced to retire from running because of arthritis in my feet so I knew it was going to be tough trying to run another marathon. I decided to be focused in my training and do just five weeks of race-specific training, having done lots of cross training in my gym at home. In those five weeks I ran 60, 70, 80, 75 and 60 miles per week and couldn't believe how quickly I got back into running. The fitness came back really quickly and I even managed three track sessions – more than ten years since I had last been on a track! Race day came and it felt really strange being treated as a celebrity rather than an athlete. I decided to run easy up to 20 miles and then, if I felt good, to push on from there. I was also worried that my foot might not last the distance – since my longest run had been 16 miles. I found it really difficult to run slowly as my instinct is always to push hard and race – still today! Because I was running more slowly, I found the distance longer than usual but at least this made me appreciate those who run for five–six hours. Now I can understand why thousands of fun runners want to take part in events like this. It's great fun...but never again!

Soon after arriving in Woking on the morning of the race, I discovered that four top Kenyan athletes were running. Apparently, they were due to compete in the Los Angeles Marathon that weekend but had been unable to get visas to travel from London to the States, so were stuck in Britain and looking for competition. I was glad that I had eased down to be sufficiently fresh to take them on! With the added incentive of chasing my own course record from two years previously, I ran away to victory in a time of 46:29, beating the old record by just six seconds. It was a nice tonic to my build-up, with an even harder three-week cycle of training ahead of me.

TRAINING FOR THE OLYMPIC MARATHON
ATLANTA, AUGUST 1996

Six months before the 1996 Olympic Marathon I arrived in Boulder, Colorado, to start my preparation for the race. I moved into an apartment with two other running friends, Jon Brown and Tommy Ratcliffe.

KEEPING GOOD COMPANY

Over the next seven weeks the three of us enjoyed each other's company and had a good spell of training together. We often ran with a group of Kenyans who were living in the same block of apartments. We had a physiotherapist on-hand to give us regular treatment. While there, we came into contact with the German coach Dieter Hogan, who passed on to us his ideas on marathon training. Dieter was coach and partner to Uta Pippig, who at the time was ranked number one in the world at the marathon. His coaching expertise had developed from working alongside the coach to Waldemar Cierpinski, who had won the Olympic marathon in 1976 and 1980. More recently, his coaching skills had helped Uta achieve a string of marathon victories, including wins in Berlin and Boston and a 2:21:45 clocking.

As my marathon career had progressed, I felt increasingly able to handle greater volumes of training. Between 1989 and 1992 my weekly mileage as an international 10,000m runner had been around 110–120 miles. From 1993 onwards I had started to reach higher weekly volumes, regularly exceeding 130 miles of running per week and occasionally covering as much as 150 miles per week. Clearly, there had had to be some trade-off between quality and quantity: though my endurance had developed, I had found it increasingly difficult to retain my speed over shorter distances. All my best times for distances between 3km and 10km had been set in 1993 or earlier.

FINDING THE RIGHT BALANCE

Dieter's training regime included conventional components of marathon training, such as sessions at 10km pace (e.g. 7 × 1 mile or 10 × 1km), fartlek and strides over 100–400m, and long runs over 20–25 miles. The emphasis of Dieter's training approach, however, lay with the continuous tempo runs of 15km and 25km. Dieter reasoned that these sustained efforts, more than any other form of training, came closest to simulating the demands of the marathon. The aim of these workouts was to increase the pace gradually over the course of the run, so that towards the end of the session we were running at – or faster than – marathon-race speed. (This same principle was also applied to some of the longer 25-mile runs, especially in the latter stage of a marathon build-up.) Taken together with the 10km training sessions, Dieter's programme ensured that neither speed nor endurance was neglected. The only question was whether we would be able to cope with the overall intensity of the training load.

Knowing how tough his own methods were, Dieter regularly gave out instructions on how we should eat, drink, and rest to enable us to cope with the training. Coming from a tradition where the path to high achievement had been narrowed down to a precise science, much attention was paid to detail. Admittedly, there were occasions when Dieter failed to appreciate important cultural differences – such as when he tried to persuade the Kenyan runners to use wholemeal flour (not widely available in Kenya) to make their *ugali*! But on the whole, much of what Dieter preached seemed to make sense. More importantly, his results demonstrated that his methods worked.

By the end of my first seven weeks, I was beginning to feel a different athlete to the one who had been seen trailing miserably behind Jon, my training partner, in a session during the early weeks of our stay. My confidence had been restored, and after an eight-month break from competition I got ready to run my first race since having surgery the previous autumn. (The background to this injury is given in Chapter 7, p. 144–147.) On my return to Britain, I ran a series of road races to test my fitness. I quickly discovered how well things were going when, in a half-marathon in Paris in mid-April, I recorded a personal best time of 1:01:06.

Sensing how well my training had gone during my seven weeks in Boulder, I planned a second stint of training there for the main part of my final three-month build-up to the Olympic Marathon later that summer.

COUNTDOWN TO ATLANTA

I started my build-up in earnest 12 weeks before the marathon. I spent the first two weeks training in Marlborough, where Bruce and Sue's assistance enabled me to recreate some of the benefits – in the form of coaching support and massage – of the training-camp environment. I then flew back out to Boulder for a block of eight weeks' training at altitude. En route I had an overnight stop in Atlanta, which gave me the chance to have another run over the marathon course.

The summer in Colorado was a far cry from the snow and icy cold we had experienced earlier in the year. Now, temperatures would rise regularly into the mid-thirties, which helped me develop the habit of replacing lost fluids during and after training.

During the next two months my training progressed better than I could have hoped. Six weeks prior to the marathon I ran a half-marathon in similar conditions to those expected in Atlanta. In a close sprint-finish I just failed to win the race, but in view of the hilly nature of the course still felt pleased with my finishing time of 1:03:01. I returned to Boulder for the final phase of hard training. The schedule for those final three weeks at altitude was tougher than any I had previously experienced. I knew I was taking risks in exploring new limits to my training capacity. For instance, over one four-day period I did two 22-mile long runs and a 10km speed workout of 7 × 1 mile. (*See* Table 3.2.)

Using the time between the hard sessions to rest and recover as best I could, I somehow managed to get through the training without breaking

TABLE 3.2 COMPARISON OF WEEKLY TRAINING CYCLES – BUILD-UP TO HALF-MARATHON AND MARATHON

7-day training cycle – build-up to half-marathon (April 1996)			7-day training cycle – build-up to marathon (August 1996)		
DAY		SESSION	DAY		SESSION
1	a.m.	35km long run	1	a.m.	35km long run
2	a.m.	15km easy	2	a.m.	18km easy
	p.m.	15km steady			8 km steady + strides
3	a.m.	16km steady	3	Early a.m.	8km easy
	p.m.	11km easy + strides		a.m.	7 × 1 miles, 3 mins recovery
				p.m.	10km easy
4	a.m.	15km tempo run	4	a.m.	35km long run
	p.m.	8km easy			
5	a.m.	25km steady	5	a.m.	14km easy
	p.m.	12km steady		p.m.	10km easy
6	a.m.	17km steady	6	a.m.	16km steady
	p.m.	8km easy		p.m.	9km easy + strides
7	a.m.	5 × 1 miles, 2 mins recovery	7	Early a.m.	8km easy
	p.m.	10km easy		a.m.	25km tempo run
		Total 120 miles			**Total 130 miles**

down. At the start of my taper, 2½ weeks prior to the race, I began to feel stronger and more determined than ever before.

The final part of my preparation and an account of the race in Atlanta are described in Chapter 5, pp. 106–109.

PEAKING FOR THE LONDON MARATHON
LONDON, APRIL 1997

By the end of 1996 I had run six marathons, four of which were championship races. My record included a win in the 1993 World Cup Marathon, fifth place in the 1996 Olympic Marathon in Atlanta, and a personal best time of 2:10:03. Top of my list of priorities for the post-Olympic year was to improve my best time for the distance. Having never yet run in Britain's premier road race, there was no better occasion on which to attempt this than the 1997 London Marathon.

I had been over the London Marathon course many times previously – twice on the back of a motorbike when I had worked for the BBC commentary team, and on other occasions when I had trained on stretches of the course. Once, at 5a.m. on a rainy, wind-swept Sunday in late October, I had run the first 21 miles of the marathon route with my wife Gail following behind in the car. Now, for the first time, I would be racing over the complete course – every mile of which, unlike any other marathon I had run, would be very familiar to me.

PREPARATION
In my preparation for the Olympic Marathon during the summer of 1996, I had discovered new limits to my training (*see* pp. 106–109). The challenge now was to reproduce that form for my debut in London. After getting married and moving house to Teddington in September 1996, I returned to training at the start of October. As the winter approached I made my customary trip to Kenya for a spell of altitude training, and on my return home in mid-January I ran a couple of cross-country races to see how my fitness was progressing. Then, with 10 weeks remaining to the marathon, I started to focus my energies on preparing for the race in London.

Aware of the demands of heavy marathon training, I planned to do the bulk of my hard training in a training camp, away from the distractions of home. In the second week of February I headed out to the Italian Olympic Training Centre at Tirrenia on the Mediterranean.

During the months of December and January my training had been geared towards cross-country races over 10km. Out in Italy I started to shift the emphasis towards greater volumes of training, and sessions of tempo running that would get me used to the sustained effort required in running a marathon. The following seven weeks were divided into two blocks of training, each comprising a phase of hard training followed by one recovery week. The first phase of hard training lasted three weeks. Each week a long run of between 2¼ and 2¾ hours; a session designed to improve my speed over 10km; and a tempo run over an extended distance (see Table 3.3).

At the end of this block of training I returned home for a week of easy training followed by a 10-mile road race in Woking (see also p. 66). Two days after the race I was back in Tirrenia for the second phase of hard training.

RACE SIMULATION

The key sessions over the following three weeks involved doing a lot of running at marathon race speed (see Table 3.4). To ensure that I did not overdo the training at this stage, there still had to be a variety of paces at which I trained. But the nearer I got to the race, the more I wanted to rehearse the kind of

TABLE 3.3 THE FIRST PHASE OF MARATHON-SPECIFIC TRAINING

WEEK	HARD SESSIONS	WEEKLY MILEAGE
1	10km cross-country race, 22 miles-long run, 25km tempo run	104
2	29 miles-long run, 20km tempo run, 15km fartlek	150
3	24 miles-long run, 3 × 6km road, 8 × 1km grass/track	132

TABLE 3.4 THE SECOND PHASE – TRAINING AT MARATHON RACE PACE

WEEK	HARD SESSIONS	WEEKLY MILEAGE
4	35km long run, then 6 easy days before race	95
5	10 mile race, 39km long run, 20km tempo run	140
6	40km long run, 10 × 1km track, 25km tempo run	152
7	41km long run, 5 easy days, 30km tempo run	106
8	15km tempo run, 20 × 400m track	108

effort and imagine the kind of tiredness that I would need to endure in the marathon itself.

In the week after my race in Woking, I did a sustained hard effort over 20km where the tempo alternated between a 'fast' (3:00 min/km) pace and a 'cruise' (3:12 min/km) pace – since my target race pace for the marathon was 3:02 min/km. The following week I ran the last 10km of the 40km long run in 32:20 (3:14 min/km), which, in the context of a heavy period of training, simulated race-pace effort. My last hard session in Tirrenia was a 25km tempo run at progressively faster speeds, starting at 3:14 min/km (16:10 for the first 5km) and finishing at 3:01 min/km (15:05 for the last 5km).

When this second phase of hard training was over (at the start of Week 7), there were just under four weeks to go to the race. I returned home and had a few days of easy running before attempting two more tough sessions. Three weeks before the marathon I ran a 30km time trial in 1:32:18 (under 2:10:00 marathon pace). Four days later I ran a 15km tempo run on dirt and road, including five 2km to 1km pace changes, in 44:46.

I now knew I was in great shape. Assuming my final two weeks of preparation went well, I would be ready to perform at my best in London.

The final stage of preparation for competition is the topic of Chapter 5 (pp. 93–109); the outcome of my race in London is described in Chapter 6 (pp. 111–131).

04

Haile Gebrselassie cools off in the 2011 Berlin Marathon

LIFESTYLE MATTERS

DIET, REST AND RECOVERY

'Training,' one American coach once told me, 'is a 24-hour proposition.' Even if you struggle to live up to this standard, you can still heed the idea behind the words: if you want to get the most out of your running, you need to think about how your style of living fits around your running.

Very few of you will become full-time professional athletes for whom running is your life. On the other hand, if you're serious about your quest for fitness, then your whole approach to training has to become more than just an occasional hobby – and certainly so in the build-up to a marathon. It has to become part of your everyday routine, even if this pattern of living lasts only for a short while. This chapter looks at two important aspects of life outside training – diet and rest – that can contribute significantly to successful athletic performance. It is outside the scope of this book to give comprehensive information on sports nutrition – only the basic principles are addressed here. For more detailed advice, refer to a good sports nutrition guide, such as *The Complete Guide to Sports Nutrition* by Anita Bean (A & C Black).

EAT WELL, TRAIN WELL

You require energy to live, and you need even more of it when you start to train hard. At its most basic level, this explains why you need to pay attention to your diet as a marathon runner. The more you train, the more food you need to eat. Remember the African saying: 'an empty sack won't stand up'.

However, a good diet is not just about eating the right quantity of food. You should also be eating a wide range of the right kind of foods. In this regard also, the African runner sets us a good example by following a diet that is high in carbohydrate, low in fat, and includes moderate amounts of protein. The pattern of their diet is ideal for providing the energy needs necessary for world-class performance.

> **'Remember the African saying:
> "an empty sack won't stand up"'**

A healthy diet has much in common with a good training regime, in the following ways.

- First, eating well should become part of your routine. Adopting a good diet – eating a piece of fruit at every meal, for example, or using semi-skimmed milk in place of whole milk – should be as commonplace as showering and stretching after your morning run.
- Second, vary your diet. Just as you need to do a variety of sessions in training to prepare for a marathon, so when it comes to diet you need to eat a wide range of good foods. There's no such thing as the one best meal for runners. It's more a matter of getting the right balance in the overall pattern of your eating.
- Third, be sensible about what you can and can't eat. Apply the same commonsense approach to your diet as you do to your training. It's not good to exist solely on chocolate or ice cream, but there's no harm in eating them in moderation. It's more important to eat enough of the right kind of foods than deny yourself those small sweet things that – taken in moderation – will not adversely affect your performance.

WHAT IS THE RUNNER'S DIET?

To answer this question, it's first important to have some basic understanding of how the body's fuel system works. Your body's energy requirements are met by two main sources: fat and carbohydrate. In the chemical reactions that take place within your body to produce energy (known as the ATP metabolic pathway), carbohydrate – or glycogen, the form in which it is stored in your body – is more immediately available than fat to meet your energy needs. This puts a premium on replenishing your glycogen stores both during and after bouts of hard training.

To do this you need first to ensure that your diet contains a good supply of carbohydrates – around 60–70 per cent of your energy intake. When I was in hard training, or during the so-called 'carbo-loading' phase of a marathon build-up (see p. 79), I aimed to eat about 600g of carbohydrate per day – or roughly 10g per day for every kg of body weight. In more routine training, the amount may have been around 400–500g, which is still considerably above that found in the average western diet (200–300g). Popular sources of carbohydrate-rich foods are bread, pasta, potatoes, rice and breakfast cereal.

Second, you should consider taking glucose-rich drinks during your long runs in training and in the marathon itself to conserve your stores of glycogen.

Remember that low levels of glycogen will require your body to utilise fat as fuel; and because of the relatively low rate at which fat can be used by the working muscles, this will cause you to slow down.

Beware, however, of adopting too extreme a solution. You may shed a few more pounds in weight by reducing the amount of fat in your diet, but some fat is needed by your body for the process of muscle repair. So a small amount of fat – between 10–20 per cent of your energy intake for the serious athlete – is both inevitable and essential in a healthy diet.

Certain fats are better for you than others. Cut down on foods that are high in saturated fats – such as crisps, biscuits, fried food, full-fat dairy produce, butter and sauces such as mayonnaise – but be more relaxed about consuming the kind of unsaturated fats found in fish and plants (e.g. olive oil, sunflower seed oil).

The remaining 15–20 per cent of your diet should be made up of protein. Proteins play an important part in your body's process of recovery after intense training. Again, it comes down to a question of variety and balance in your diet. You may be able to get your daily protein requirements from eating a large steak every day, but this might also result in you comsuming too much fat and not enough carbohydrate. In addition to meat and poultry, good supplies of protein are found in fish, milk and cheese, eggs and pulses (e.g. tofu and soya beans).

Unlike racehorse jockeys before a race, or boxers before their next bout, runners in training don't need to watch their weight too carefully. If you are overweight at the start of your training programme, you will soon begin to shed pounds as you take more exercise. Once you have discovered an optimum training weight, it may then be helpful to check your weight on a weekly basis to ensure that you are neither eating too much nor too little (*see* above).

Remember also the importance of drinking after exercise. Dehydration can occur from having drunk too little either before or during the course of training. For every hour of exercise you should aim to drink 1 -1½ litres over and above your normal amount. (This amount should increase if you are training in unusually warm weather.) A dark yellow colour in your urine, coupled often with a significant loss of weight, is a sign that you aren't drinking enough.

The great thing about being a runner is that you burn off lots of calories when you exercise. This means that you should be eating more than the average sedentary person and that you need not become obsessed with the exact quantities of different types of food that you are eating. The key thing is to develop healthy habits in your overall pattern of shopping, cooking and eating. Eating well will make you feel good and at the same time benefit your training.

FITTING MEALS AROUND EXERCISE

Just as you need to plan when you are going to train, so too you need to think about when you are going to eat – both before and after exercise. The rule of thumb is not to eat anything in the two-hour period before going out for a run, and if this is a larger meal it's better to leave a gap of three to four hours. Many runners find that an early morning run before breakfast is a good time to train, or in the early evening before dinner. Conversely, don't deprive yourself of food for the whole day and then expect to feel good on your evening run. If you do prefer to train in the second half of the day, make sure you have a good breakfast and if necessary an easily digestible snack later on so as to maintain your energy levels throughout the day.

POST-EXERCISE NUTRITION

Having accepted that there's no magic food that will make you run faster, it's still worth considering how your diet can contribute to your performance. For instance, the best way to speed recovery after a hard bout of training is to start the refuelling process within the first two hours (and preferably within the first hour) of finishing exercise. Try to develop the habit of following your run with at least a small snack (e.g. some toast, or a piece of cake or muffin) and a large glass of water or juice. Bananas are also popular among runners wanting to replenish their energy stores quickly and efficiently. If you're training away from home, it may be useful to take with you a small post-run snack (e.g. some fruit or an energy bar and a drink) which will help revive you after exercise and keep you going until your next proper meal.

SAMPLE MEAL PLAN – 1 DAY OF MARATHON TRAINING

- Breakfast: glass of orange juice, cereal + banana + semi-skimmed milk, toast + margarine (or other low-fat spread) + honey/marmalade, tea/coffee
- Morning snack:* apple, fruit tea
- Lunch: sandwich of ham/cheese + tomato, low-fat yoghurt, kiwi fruit, glass of water
- Afternoon snack:* English muffin + jam, cup of tea
- Dinner: Spinach leaf salad, grilled fish + rice + broccoli, slice of carrot cake and camomile tea

*Snacks optional depending on time of workout and phase of training

PRE-RACE CARBO-LOADING
'Carbo-loading' before a marathon*

It is crucial that you start your marathon with maximal reserves of glycogen. This is because the amount of glycogen that your body can access from its reserves in the course of a marathon may actually be less than you need to complete a marathon. Your body accounts for the shortfall partly by drawing on fat as a source of fuel – providing about ten per cent of the energy requirement for elite athletes, and rising to nearer 50 per cent among slower runners – and partly by using supplementary amounts of carbohydrate that you consume while running your marathon (*see* below).

Building up your carbohydrate reserves before a race is known as 'carbo-loading'. Although the term is commonly associated with pasta parties on the evening before a marathon, the process should start about three days before your race. If your marathon is on a Sunday, lunch and dinner on both the Friday and Saturday should be carbohydrate-rich meals. The emphasis should be on eating a good helping of carbohydrate, but not stuffing yourself or overeating to the extent that you are left with a bloated feeling when you go to the start. When carbo-loading, you should also take on board plenty of fluid – without this, your body is unable to fill your glycogen stores.

Pre-race eating

It's important to be careful about your diet before racing – or indeed, before a particularly hard workout. The intensity of effort involved in racing, coupled with the nervous tension that accompanies any competitive situation, can unsettle your stomach. Planning your eating around your running is made easier by the fact that most road races, like nearly all marathons, are held in the morning: assuming that you've had a good dinner in the evening before the race, you won't need to eat much on race-day morning. Your pre-race breakfast won't actually help your performance; but it's equally important that you don't start the race on an empty stomach. I usually have something simple like a glass of fruit juice, followed by a couple of pieces of toast and honey together with a cup of tea, but these should be taken about three hours before the start of the race. If it's warm, it's important to have drunk plenty of water – perhaps as much as 2–3 litres – the previous day, and to have 'topped up' on the

---

* A small minority of elite marathon runners no longer use the method of carbo-loading before a marathon. Either they have reservations about eating too much in the period leading up to the event, or they feel confident that in the course of regular hard training they have learned how to refuel adequately after exhausting their glycogen stores. However, the practice of carbo-loading – as I advocate here – is still common among first-time marathon runners and non-elite runners.

---

morning of the race. Rarely will you end up drinking too much – and if you do, you will simply pee out the excess.

DRINKING ON THE RUN

In your kit-bag, which will accompany you to the start of your marathon, you should include a carbohydrate sports drink. Starting two hours – and up until thirty minutes – before the start of a marathon, I regularly take small sips of this drink. (Stopping half an hour beforehand will give you time to pee out any excess fluid.) I then usually take a final 'top-up' of around 50ml about five

VIEW FROM THE ROAD
Pierre Monroy: Learning the hard way about food and drink for the marathon

Pierre Monroy learns the hard way about fuelling for the marathon
Even though for many people running a marathon may be a lifetime goal, it's not always easy finding out how best to prepare for it. You can probably get some useful advice by reading books or going on the internet, but in the end what seems to really count is what you learn from your own personal experience. When I ran my first marathon in Nairobi, high altitude was not a problem since I was living in Addis Ababa. But I still had to think about the local weather conditions in Nairobi (which are generally hotter than in Addis) as well as another key factor – what I needed to eat – which previously had not been important when running 10km races. I say this because in the build up to the marathon we ran the big 10km race in Addis – just because it was a race not to be missed. For my marathon, a race over 20 or 25km would have been better but there wasn't one around. My one big mistake was that in the race I should have used energy drinks and energy bars throughout, but I didn't do this – partly because I hadn't realised how important this was, and partly because these weren't made available for runners there. In fact the only energy we found was some sugar which was being handed out in the last 10km of the race. The outcome was that I ran a rather disappointing 4 hours and 15 minutes – pretty slow, but at least I was pleased to get to the finish. What I learned in that race was that you should not wait until you are thirsty or exhausted before you take on food or drink. I would add that only well-trained runners can handle this distance: the idea that you can prepare seriously for a marathon off three sessions per week is just a myth.

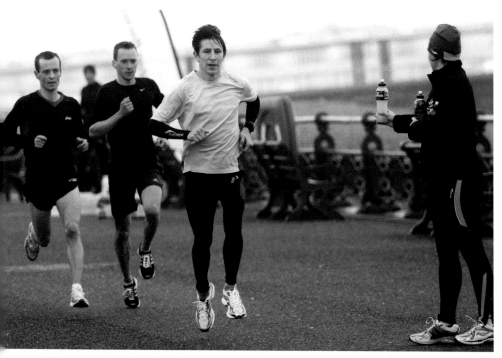

Elite runners practise taking drinks during training

minutes before the start. In this way I ensure that my carbohydrate and fluid reserves are replete on the point of starting my marathon.

During the marathon it is important to drink regularly at the various 'feed' stations along the route. I aim to drink between 100 and 150ml of fluid every 5km throughout the race. For this I use a carbohydrate drink with a dilution of roughly 10g/100ml. But whether you drink water or one of the commercial sports drinks, your motto should be: 'Drink little and often.' Don't wait for thirst to arrive – if you do, this is a sign that you are already badly dehydrated. And don't be fooled if your marathon takes place in relatively cool conditions. Obviously, you won't need to drink quite as much as in hot weather; but you will still lose a lot of fluid in covering the distance, and drinking on the run is one sure way of improving your chances of keeping going to the finish.

Practice makes perfect

None of the procedures I have described above should be attempted for the first time on race day itself. You should try out various routines in the course of your build-up and find the one that suits you best. This is especially so when it comes to drinking while on the run. In training this might involve running a looped circuit that allows you to pick up a drinks bottle every 30 minutes. It's even better if you can find a friend to cycle alongside you and pass you drinks at regular intervals. By marathon day, you should have decided exactly what you will eat and drink before and during the race.

REST AND RECOVERY

The harder you train, the greater the stress you place on your body. The greater the stress, the more likely you are to break down with an injury or illness. If you do succumb to a running-related injury, you will start to learn the process of respecting your own body's limitations. This in turn should make you more aware of the importance of rest and recovery in the overall structure of your training.

In the course of preparing for a marathon, your determination to get through the training sometimes makes it hard to sense when you are doing too much. Many runners simply complain of 'feeling tired all the time'. In these moments it becomes even more important to check that you are giving your body time to recover from intense bouts of exercise as well as from the

DIETARY SUPPLEMENTS

Below is a list of some of the ergogenic aids (legal substances, commonly accepted to be performance-enhancing) that I use regularly:

- Carbohydrate drinks: to replenish glycogen stores during and after training and competition
- Isotonic drinks: to replace important minerals lost (e.g. through sweat) in training and competition – these are especially useful in hot conditions
- Iron supplements: to ensure adequate iron reserves. Low levels of iron restrict your body's ability to produce haemoglobin, in turn limiting your body's oxygen-carrying capacity
- Vitamin C: taken in tablet form as a supplement to intake of Vitamin C from food, to boost the immune system, thus protecting against illness
- Glutamine: taken in powdered form dissolved in water, may aid process of rebuilding damaged cells in muscles, thus improving rate of recovery and reducing chance of infection after prolonged or intense exercise
- Branched-chain amino acids: taken as drink solution, may affect mental agility and perception of fatigue during sustained physical exercise.

cumulative effects of hard training and high mileage. High levels of stress from training, combined with other stresses in your daily routine, place unusually high demands on your body. If you don't give yourself time to recover from these stresses, the likely result will be breakdown. Put simply, if you want to train harder, you might have to rest harder.

REST AS TRAINING

Strange as it may seem, rest is a vital ingredient of a good training programme. This is not meant as a 'cop-out'; rather, it is a way of saying that sometimes you will actually benefit more from *not* over-exerting yourself. Consider these various practices:

- When you are feeling worn-out from training, it may be better to have one or two days of no running. The world's best distance runners sometimes take a day off to rejuvenate themselves, even when it's not prescribed in their training programme.
- If you're unsure whether you're ready to do your next hard session, first see how you feel during your warm-up. It's not too late to decide after 15 minutes of easy running – and if you're still in doubt, play safe and give yourself another day to recover.
- Don't be afraid of doing some of your recovery runs at a snail's pace. It often makes more sense to run slowly when you're tired, rather than to push yourself into a state of long-term fatigue.
- Arrange to do some of your steady runs with a training partner who runs slightly slower than you, if this will prevent you from over-exerting yourself*. Doing this once or twice a week will not lead to a loss of fitness. Indeed, it should make you feel even stronger for your harder workouts.

In addition to changes in your eating patterns, another way of ensuring that you start your marathon with high glycogen levels is by resting for the three to four days leading up to the event. Running training should be kept to a minimum – a couple of easy runs, of 20 minutes each – and where possible you should avoid being on your feet for long periods on the day before the race (for example, walking around pre-race marathon Expo events).

It is equally important that you plan easy weeks into an overall training programme. Plan to take at least one easy week in every six weeks of training

---

* This can also be achieved by wearing a heart-rate monitor during your recovery runs, and ensuring that your heart rate stays below a set limit (e.g. 70–75 per cent of your maximum heart rate).

– and more regularly if the training is particularly hard. If you are a regular runner, you should think about taking at least one month of minimal training at least once in the year (*see* also Chapter 8, pp. 151–161).

Incorporating rest and recovery into your training programme might also include:

- taking a few days of rest when you pick up a small injury. You will not lose much fitness by having a few days off running. If you're keen enough, you might even be able to maintain fitness during this break from running by switching to some form of low-impact training such as swimming or cycling

Foil blankets are often used to keep runners warm at the end of a marathon

- following a hard training session with a hot shower and stretch, coupled with a cup of tea and a piece of cake, rather than simply crashing out on the sofa as soon as you stagger in exhausted through the door
- breaking a long car journey to stretch for 5–10 minutes to avoid feeling really stiff when you get to the other end.

KEY POINTS
- Incorporate a healthy diet into your everyday routine
- Pay more attention to eating the right kind of food, rather than worrying about how much you are eating
- Make sure that you are drinking plenty, especially when training in warm weather
- Start the process of post-exercise recovery by consuming a snack within an hour of finishing training
- Recognise the importance of rest in your overall pattern of training.

Rest means different things to different people. For some, it may mean getting a few more hours of sleep; for others, it may involve putting your feet up for half an hour in the middle of the day. For those of you who can only dream of such luxuries, it may simply involve cutting back on your social activities. Whatever your situation, fitting rest into your programme – and thus getting the most out of your running – requires discipline and good organisation. It will also depend on your priorities in life. If something is important enough to you, you will make every effort to make it happen.

USEFUL TIPS
Measures for post-race recovery

To prevent you from suffering too many after-effects of running a marathon – and thus enabling you to enjoy your post-race feeling of satisfaction – you should take certain precautions once the race is over. By the time you reach the finish you will have run down many of your normal defences against illness: your body is both short of energy and dehydrated. In addition, your muscles will be sore and in need of repair. So, having crossed the line and got your finishing medal – even if you've sworn never to run another marathon – what should you do next?

In the immediate aftermath of the race, you should:

- stay warm – once you stop running, you will lose body heat quickly, so put on a tracksuit or sweat top as soon as you can after finishing
- start replenishing your reserves by drinking plenty and even eating small snacks – the longer you leave it before refuelling, the wearier you will become. Even if you're too tired to think about food or drink so soon after finishing, remember that your body needs desperately to rebuild its energy stores
- try if you can to walk for 10 minutes, rather than collapsing in a heap after reaching the finish. This will go some way to getting rid of the waste products that are likely to cause stiffness and soreness afterwards
- aim to get into a hot bath as soon as conveniently possible.

In the days following your marathon, the best form of recuperation is rest combined with some light exercise (especially walking) and gentle stretching. Even if you feel that your energy levels have returned to normal, you should resist the temptation of attempting any hard training for at least one week (and preferably longer) after the marathon. This will allow time for your muscle cells and tissues to repair, and thus give you more chance of resuming effective training in the long term. The process of recovery and repair can be helped by having a massage – alternatively, go for a swim or Jacuzzi. Continue to eat well.

TABLE 4.1 POST-MARATHON RECOVERY PERIODS

Marathon	Weekly mileage (two weeks post-race)	Resumption of normal training (post-race)	Date of first race post-marathon
Hamburg, May 1993	45 miles 92 miles	2 weeks	6 weeks
San Sebastian, October 1993	67 miles 72 miles	5 weeks	6 weeks
Helsinki, August 1994	72 miles 100 miles	2 weeks	10 weeks
Atlanta, August 1996	40 miles 65 miles	8 weeks	8 weeks
London, April 1997	6 miles 11 miles	3 weeks	11 weeks

VIEW FROM THE ROAD
Jane Thomson: Running in London

Jane Thomson becomes a London Marathon finisher

I ran my first marathon in Edinburgh in 2009, my second in Kielder in 2010 and my third in London in 2011. I'm relatively new to running, having only started in 2005 at the age of 29. In my first few years I was a member of York Knavesmire Harriers; now I train with the Dragons Club in Yeadon. I remember clearly my London Marathon experience. Anticipation and excitement mixed with nervousness: had I eaten and drunk enough to get me through the race; did I have enough gels with me and would I be able to stomach them and what about now – do I need another trip to the loo? When we got going, the spectators were amazing and the miles seemed to pass very quickly. Around mile 19 I 'hit the wall' and it suddenly got much harder. I even started to struggle with the noise of the crowd. But I reached the finish, helped on by the shouts of a few familiar faces over the last few miles, and managed to cross the finish line in 4 hours and 54 minutes. It was a great feeling to finish and ever since it's been great to say 'I've done the London Marathon!'

TABLE 4.2 RECOVERY AND RESUMPTION OF TRAINING AFTER 1997 LONDON MARATHON

WEEKS 1 & 2		WEEK 3	
Sunday	Marathon	Sunday	13 miles easy
Monday	Swim + massage	Monday a.m.	6 miles easy + gym Monday p.m. 6 miles easy
Tuesday	20 min jog + massage	Tuesday a.m.	6 miles easy + strides Tuesday p.m. 6 miles steady
Wednesday a.m.	30 min jog	Wednesday	13 miles easy + gym
Wednesday p.m.	Fly to Crete		
Thursday week 1 to Friday week 2	8-day walking holiday (no running)	Thursday a.m.	20 × 150m short hills
		Thursday p.m.	6 miles easy
		Friday	9 miles easy + gym
Saturday a.m.	45 min easy run	Saturday a.m.	10 miles steady
Saturday p.m.	35 min easy run	Saturday p.m.	5 miles easy + strides
Total (week 1) (excluding race)	6 miles	Total (week 3)	88 miles
Total (week 2)	11 miles		

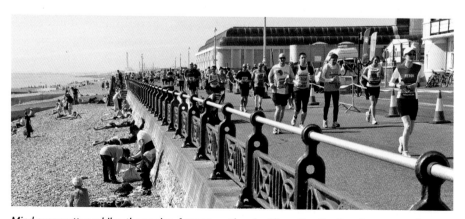

Mind over matter: while others relax, for runners there's still another 3 miles of tarmac to the finish of the Brighton Marathon

THE EUROPEAN CHAMPIONSHIPS
HELSINKI, AUGUST 1994

COURSE 'RECCE'

The small Finnish town of Punkalaidun, two hours' drive from Helsinki, was where I started my race preparation for the 1994 European Championship Marathon. It was there, three months before the opening of the championships, that I ran a 5000m track race prior to starting my marathon build-up. The main reason, however, for my trip to Finland at this stage in my preparation was to enable me to have a look at the Helsinki marathon course.

Following the best tradition of Finnish javelin throwing, the Punkalaidun race organisers had invited Steve Backley, Britain's former javelin world record holder, to compete at their meeting against some of the top Finnish throwers. Sadly, both for the organisers and the local crowd, injury had forced Steve to withdraw at the last moment. Their loss was my gain, as I was offered the courtesy car that had been made available for him! After the race I spent a day in Helsinki and did a couple of runs on the marathon course. A Finnish television company wanted some footage for a preview of the championships and in exchange for a 20-minute interview they offered to drive me around the course. By the end of my short visit, I felt that I had been well looked after by my Finnish friends.

RACE REHEARSALS

After a 25-day period of altitude training at Font Romeu in the French Pyrenees, I finished my hardest block of training for the marathon 3½ weeks before the race and returned home to make final preparations. The first priority on returning home was to take a few days of easy running to recover from the exertions of previous training. Once I was feeling fresh again, I did my last long run before the marathon. Three weeks to the day before the marathon, I ran 22½ miles over a four-lap course that I had devised on the roads around Marlborough. Each 9km circuit included a couple of hilly sections, thus replicating the Helsinki marathon course that was also being run over a four-lap course. It also allowed me to practise taking drinks at regular intervals. Bruce and Sue were on hand to arrange the drinks table, refilling my bottles and giving me encouragement during the run.

Over the next couple of weeks I rehearsed a number of aspects of my race-day routine. On days when I was doing hard efforts, for instance, I had an early breakfast and then trained three hours later – just as I would be doing on the morning of the marathon. I also did some more practice of drinking while on the run.

In my final race two weeks before the marathon, at the Great Welsh Run 10km in Cardiff, I finished a close second behind Paul Evans with a personal best time for 10km on the road of 28:25. Two days later I flew to Helsinki and went straight to the training camp at Solvalla, a short journey from the Finnish capital, which I had visited previously during my course 'recce' in May. Although Solvalla would be my base for the 12 days leading up to the race, I also planned to spend three nights in the Athletes' Village in the final week before the race.

SCANDINAVIAN SUMMER

Training at Solvalla in the warm Scandinavian sunshine allowed me to acclimatise to the conditions that we were likely to experience in the race. Strangely enough, it had been a warm summer in Britain that year; but knowing how changeable the British weather could be, I hadn't wanted to take any chances when making my plans. The further advantage of staying in a training camp was that I was away from the distractions of home, with plenty of time to rest and rehearse my race plans – mentally more than physically. Bruce and Sue were also there to support me. They understood exactly what I was there for and brimmed with excitement about what lay ahead. At the same time we could enjoy relaxing together once the training was over.

Seven days before the men's marathon, the women's marathon took place. This gave me the chance to see the set-up being used for the drinks stations

CARBO-LOADING BEFORE THE HELSINKI MARATHON

- **Thursday lunchtime:** pasta meal + bread/jam + carbo drink
- **Thursday p.m. post-run:** bread roll + banana + carbo drink
- **Thursday dinner:** (two bowls of) rice + meat sauce + bread + apple + carbo drink
- **Friday breakfast:** porridge + banana + toast/honey + juice/tea
- **Friday lunchtime:** potatoes/broccoli + tomato sauce + cake + carbo drink
- **Friday p.m. post-run:** High Five energy bar + drink
- **Friday evening:** (large plateful of) pasta + fish sauce + bread + carbo drink
- **Saturday breakfast:** as for Friday
- **Saturday lunchtime:** spaghetti bolognese + bread + drink
- **Saturday evening:** fish + rice + cake

and get a better feel for the course. After the women's marathon I moved into the Athletes' Village as the excitement of starting competition took hold in the British camp.

My last hard effort four days before the race involved 20 minutes of brisk running on part of the marathon circuit. I ran this in my racing kit, at the same time of day as the race would take place. I even warmed up in the same warm-up area that we would be using on the day of the race, to make sure I was familiar with the procedures there. After this run I moved back out to the peace and quiet of Solvalla. My hard training was over. Now it was time to rest, and to build up reserves of strength for the marathon. With three days to go before the race I started my carbo-loading diet.

My weight gain over these three days was around 5lb (or just over 2kg). I was already looking forward to my next non-pasta meal! As well as feeling that my fuel tanks were full, I also felt a great sense of readiness to perform: well prepared, well rested, and familiar with my routine for race day. This still didn't prevent me from feeling nervously excited about the prospect of trying to win the race. But I knew I had done all I could to prepare myself well for competition.

'LET BATTLE COMMENCE!'

I came into these championships carrying the mantle of pre-race favourite. My strongest opposition was likely to come from the Spanish and Portuguese runners. In winning the 1993 World Cup Marathon in San Sebastian 10 months previously, I had defeated many of Europe's best marathoners, including Spain's home favourite Diego Garcia. Garcia now came to Helsinki in search of revenge. Unbeknown to me, he had prepared for this race with two other Spanish marathon runners, Martin Fiz and Alberto Juzdado. Together they had devised a strategy to prevent me from repeating my 1993 victory.

My race plan was identical to my winning strategy in San Sebastian. Confident that none of my opponents could run faster than me over shorter distances, I hoped to stay with the leaders until 5km from home and then make a decisive break to the finish. I also made a deliberate decision not to show at the front of the field until the race's final stages. By following the pace set by the leaders, I hoped to conserve as much mental and physical energy as possible until the point in the race when I needed it most.

From the first kilometre, the German athlete Kurt Stenzel took the lead. The chasing group thought it unlikely that he would figure in the race's later stages, so were happy to continue at a relatively modest opening pace. By the end of the first of the four 10km laps, Stenzel held a 45-second lead. The group then decided to chase him. The pace quickened for the second quarter of the race, and the German was caught at the 17km point. On the third 10km lap a number of runners tried in turn to get out in front. I was content to run at a short distance off the pace as long as I could retain 'mental contact' with the leaders. At 26km I was nine seconds behind the leading group of about 10 runners, and the gap remained the same until 29km.

At this point the leading group started to split up as the Spaniards initiated another surge. I covered their move so that at 30km I had moved into sixth place, just three seconds behind the leaders. Another increase in pace ensued, and I moved up to fourth behind the three Spaniards, but still around 15m off the lead.

But this was as close as I came to the front of the race. With 11km to go to the finish, the three Spaniards ahead of me gradually started to wind up the pace. Running in tandem, they took it in turns to make the pace, glancing back every so often to see how far I was behind them. Back down the road, and running now on my own, I was unable to match their increase in tempo and started to fall behind. At 32km I was seven seconds off the lead; by 34km this gap had grown to 15 seconds; at 36km it was 24 seconds and rapidly growing. Now it was merely a question of which of the three Spaniards would lift the title. My hopes of a medal were gone.

I had been outrun over the last seven miles of the race by three quicker runners. The leaders had run 15:09 for the 5km to 35km and Fiz, the eventual winner, had run the next 5km in 15:20. But I also sensed that I had been outmanoeuvred, since I had never been allowed to get into a position from where I could use my quicker finishing speed.

The result was a big disappointment. I had missed the chance to win a major championship title. There hadn't been much wrong with my training or my final preparation, in which a good diet and adequate periods of recovery now played an integral part. I was left questioning my race strategy and what I might do to plan this out as carefully as I did my training.

Adrift in 4th place in the 1994 European Championship Marathon as the Spaniards win all three medals

91

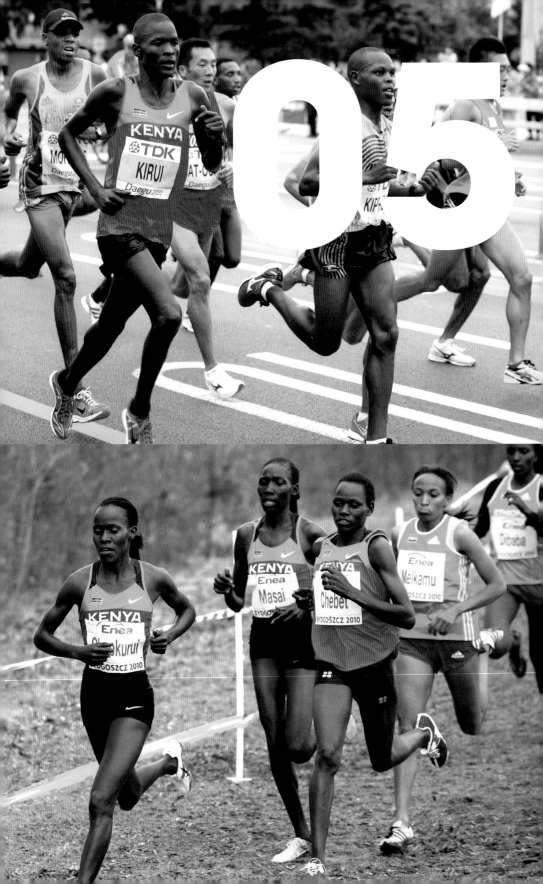

RACE PREPARATION

Your ability to achieve your marathon goals depends on a number of factors. These include:

* how well you train in the months leading up to the race
* how good you are at bringing your fitness to a peak in the weeks before the race
* how well you can get the best out of yourself on race day.

In the last three chapters I have suggested ways to help you train well in the months leading up to the race. From this you will have realised that the process of good training does not involve flogging yourself to the point of exhaustion every time you go out to exercise, but is rather the result of following a structured programme of hard workouts interspersed with easier runs and adequate recovery. In other words, it is crucial to strike the right balance between effort and stress on the one hand, and rest and recovery on the other.

No matter what your level, this same 'balancing' principle should also guide your pattern of training in the final few weeks before your marathon – the period known as the 'taper'.

TAPERING FOR A MARATHON

If you were to plot a graph of your weekly training volume over the course of a 12-week build-up, you should end up with a bell-shaped curve with the high point of the curve representing your hardest weeks of training. (Ideally, the curve should be 'skewed' to the left, indicating that your hardest

Photos opposite, from top to bottom: Kenya's Abel Kirui on his way to winning the 2011 World Championship Marathon in Daegu; Lineth Chepkurui leads eventual winner Emily Chebet at the 2010 World Cross-Country Championships in Bydgoszcz

training has occurred in the second half of your build-up.) If you have followed a pattern of hard and easy phases, you might even have two or three high points. The 'taper' – or the period in which training volume and intensity are gradually reduced in the run-up to the race – is shown on the graph where the curve 'tapers off' at the right-hand end.

Figure 5.1 Showing a race taper for a 12-week marathon build-up

For an example of a race taper, *see* Figure 5.1, which represents my training for the 1997 London Marathon. In your case the training volume is likely to be considerably less, but the overall pattern of high and low points of the curve should be similar.

Emphasis on recovery

If you overdo your training during the taper, you will still have some residual tiredness in your legs when you line up for the start of the marathon. So the emphasis at this stage in your training should be on making sure that you have recovered from all the hard training that has gone before.

There are two fundamental reasons why you need to train less, immediately prior to competition:

- so that you feel fresh and bursting with energy when you start the race
- so that your body is given time to adapt to the stress that the previous load of training has imposed on your system.

Time to adapt

Once you get stuck into the rigours of hard training – and actually start to relish that end-of-day feeling of tiredness – it's sometimes easy to fall into the trap of thinking that you are at your fittest when training at your hardest. The truth is that you will be at your fittest once you have allowed this training to take effect. To allow this to happen you need to allow yourself a period of recovery from the spell of hard training.

Remember that fitness develops from a process of stress followed by recovery. Understanding this principle is an important step towards getting your taper right for your marathon. Only by reducing your training and allowing yourself time to recover will you be able to reach a higher level of readiness to run.

Of course, it's easier said than done. In the days immediately prior to the race, when feelings of apprehension run high, it's easy to feel you ought to be doing more rather than less. Some runners even start to feel sluggish from having reduced their normal amount of training. In these moments of uncertainty you need to restrain any impulses to do more training – and so ensure that you arrive on the start line feeling well rested and ready to produce your big effort there.

Length of taper

How long should this final tapering period last? Though the time may vary according to the severity of the previous period of training, a general rule is that your body requires around two weeks to adapt to the stresses of a given block of training.

I learned this lesson after one particularly hard period of training in Kenya in 1992. This was my first attempt at training three times a day on a regular basis. The end of this two-week period of training marked the start of my taper for competition, two weeks before the World Cross-Country Championships in Boston.

Only when I started to reduce my training did I realise how tired I felt from all my hard training. I found it a struggle to do a run of 30 minutes, when a week earlier I had been putting in over 20 miles of running each day. Fortunately I had just enough time to recover in time for the race, where I finished 15th, my highest finishing position ever in these championships.

Although the race had gone well, the period of training that came after the championships – almost a month after my hard training in Kenya had finished – felt even better. With hindsight it appeared that I needed even longer to recover from my hard training than I had originally expected.

As a rule, you should try to finish your final cycle of hard training at least two weeks and not more than four weeks before the marathon. It's important to balance the need to recover from hard efforts in training with the thought that if you take things too easily in the weeks leading up to the race, you may actually lose fitness. What's more, if you lose touch with the feeling of making a hard effort, the shock of having to run 26 miles on race day might get the better of you.

Whether it is two or four weeks may also depend on whether you plan to run any races before your marathon. For instance, if you are planning to race in the final few weeks before your marathon, it's probably better to finish your hard training a bit earlier so that you are not too tired going into these races. If you're not planning to race before the marathon, your final period of hard training can finish as little as two weeks before the event.

Table 5.1 shows the different approaches I used prior to my marathons in the period 1994 to 1996. Of these four races I performed best in Atlanta,

TABLE 5.1 LENGTH OF TAPER IS OFTEN DETERMINED BY PREPARATION RACES

Marathon	End of hardest training period (weeks before marathon)	Date of preparation races (weeks before marathon)
Helsinki – 1994	3½	2
Korea – 1995	3½	2
Gothenburg – 1995	5½	5, 4 and 3
Atlanta – 1996	2½	6

when the period of my hardest training finished just 2½ weeks before the race. (Admittedly, my training throughout the entire build-up for Atlanta was superior to the other races.)

Content of the taper

As you taper for the marathon, your training should serve two purposes:

- It should aim to keep your body in a state of readiness for the tough exertions ahead. To do this you have to continue with a reasonable amount of good training, even during the course of the taper.
- While keeping up a certain level of training, you should strive to maintain a state of optimum rest and recovery – especially in the final few days leading up to the race.

To achieve this balance, think of your hard sessions as a means of maintaining rather than developing fitness. Adopt a controlled approach to these sessions and then give yourself more time to recover from them. If you are fresh when you start these sessions, you are more likely to perform well in them. Feeling good about your final workouts before the marathon should in turn boost your confidence about running well on race day.

The final two weeks before the marathon should be the time when you rehearse the feeling of running at your intended race pace. Your really long runs will have finished; now, any longer training runs should serve merely as a reminder of what is ahead of you. Resist the temptation of wanting to test out your fitness by attempting, for instance, a 20-mile run one week before your marathon. Some faster running over shorter distances will help give you a good feeling about your running, but there is not enough time for these sessions to have much effect on your fitness. So instead you should think of

TABLE 5.2 TRAINING PATTERN FOR THE TAPER

Weeks before marathon	Training load (% maximum)	Length of long run	Number of hard sessions	Key session
3	80%	Long (at least 20 miles) + drinks	2	2 x 30 mins at race pace
2	60%	1½hrs	2	3 x 10 mins at race pace
1	40%	1hr	1	2 x 1 mile at race pace

gathering up all your reserves of energy for the one 26-mile race-day effort ahead of you.

Assuming that you are not planning to race in the three weeks leading up to your marathon, Table 5.2 shows a pattern for your training during the tapering period.

Your last session of faster running should take place at least four days before the marathon. Some runners like to do some faster-paced running

VIEW FROM THE ROAD
John Britton: The final few weeks and the feeling after

John Britton made sure that his post-race beer tasted good
After my final long run three weeks before the marathon, I ran a total of about 40 miles over the next fortnight. Then in the final week I just did a couple of short three-mile runs. That felt very uncomfortable – I wanted to run every day, but should probably have done even less. I also gave up alcohol for the week before – the longest time I've done that in years – and was surprised by how much that contributed to the mental preparation. The beer after the race tasted good as well!

The physical exhaustion of the race took two weeks to wear off, much longer than the long training runs, but two weeks to the day after the race I ran faster than ever before.

EXPERT COMMENT
Geoff Wightman: The final few weeks of preparation

Geoff Wightman is Director of Run Britain

Four weeks before a marathon, I used to do my longest training run in the entire build-up – about 30 miles at a very slow pace. From that point onwards, my overall mileage came down steadily until the day of the marathon. Three weeks before the marathon, I was often starting to feel a little bit less tired from all the training and would run a half-marathon.

In the final week of training, I used a session given to me by Charlie Spedding, winner of the 1984 London Marathon, of running 5 × 400m efforts, which I usually did on the Wednesday four days before the race, just to get some zip into my legs. The funny thing was that every time I ran it I felt like a sausage dog. It became almost a superstition that I should feel terrible for this workout. I am sure it had something to do with the body starting to shut down, ready for a major effort.

The best advice I got on mental preparation for the marathon was from Alan Storey, who said that you need to get to the halfway point feeling that you are ready to race a half-marathon from then on. If you feel like you are 'hanging on' at any stage prior to that, you are going too fast.

After each of my ten marathons, I never ran a step for seven days, and it was only after two weeks that I would think about what to do next because I never quite knew how I was going to recover or how my body would react to any more strenuous exercise. Having said that, I did once manage to play a tough game of 5-a-side football the day after one marathon, but that was only because I was on such a high after qualifying to compete in an international championship competition for the first time.

(such as 8 × 400m) to produce that feeling of running comfortably at speed. I prefer to run a few repetitions at a more relaxed pace over a longer distance (such as 4 × 2km) at marathon race pace. Whatever your preference, you must ensure that this final workout is not too demanding.

In the remaining days before the race you should take things very easy, so that you feel relaxed and well rested. For some, this will mean doing a few easy runs over short distances; for others it might mean taking a few days of complete rest. As well as reducing your training, you should try to minimise your energy expenditure in other areas of your life, especially where this might normally contribute to feelings of tiredness. Your goal is to reach the end of this period feeling fresh and ready for a superhuman show of endurance.

Mental preparation

Though the physical effort of training is reduced in your taper, the final few weeks before the race may be stressful for other reasons. You may have to cope with feelings of growing excitement and/or impatience as your day of reckoning approaches. In these moments you need to reassure yourself that you have done enough training and that your relative inactivity is permitting you to reach a peak of fitness. If you can't do this yourself, maybe a coach, friend or partner can help put your mind at rest.

Visualisation

You may find that your mental preparation runs closely in parallel with the more physical aspects of training. In the course of your training you may be able to imagine yourself running the marathon, staying relaxed and in control, or conversely hanging on with grim determination as fatigue sets in. At its most basic, this is what race visualisation is all about. If you haven't thought

VIEW FROM THE ROAD
Sarah Appelhans: The correct mindset

Sarah Appelhans on celebrating a birthday with a marathon in New York

I turned 40 a few days before the 2011 New York City Marathon. I had been focusing on the race since midsummer and, as race weekend approached, I was determined to have the time of my life. Even though this was my third marathon, I still had a sense of dread, heightened by the fact that a sprained ankle which had caused me to miss several weeks of training in my build-up had still not fully healed by the time I got on the plane. I ran the first half of the race like a kid in a candy shop, taking in the amazing atmosphere of the occasion. At mile 18 I started looking out for friends I'd arranged to see, but couldn't spot them. By mile 19 I went through a real low, aware that I'd missed a much-needed morale boost, and for the next 3 or 4 miles I had to work really hard to lift the mental cloud over me. I finished the race in 3:56:14, faster than my first marathon. As I crossed the line and took my medal, thoughts of jet lag, the unbearable cold from waiting around before the start and stiff legs in the 20th mile vanished in an instant. Looking back, I realised that I had made the mistake of pinning too much hope on seeing friends, only to end up missing them. It's true that your mindset does affect your marathon experience.

about it already in the course of your training, these final few days leading up to a race are a good time to imagine yourself running your marathon and to anticipate the different situations that you are likely to confront as you do so:

- Will you be able to keep yourself from going too fast at an early stage in the race, when you are feeling full of energy?
- How will you react at the halfway stage when you begin to feel some tiredness in your legs?
- How will you cope with running in crowds of other runners?
- What will give you the determination to dig deeper into your mental and physical reserves in those final few miles of the marathon?

The better prepared you are for the situation, the more likely you are to cope when the situation arises. This heightened mental awareness about your upcoming performance should amply make up for the reduced physical stress of training in the final few days before competition.

VIEW FROM THE ROAD
Fay Sanders: Running too fast

Fay Sanders came unstuck in the 2011 Barcelona Marathon
I ran my first marathon in Athens in October 2010. It was an amazing experience. My finishing time was 4 hours and 9 minutes but after the race I had a lingering feeling that I could have run faster had I not run so slowly over the race's first half. This had happened because I had decided to run the first 18 miles with another member of my training group and he kept urging me to slow down whenever I wanted to run ahead. Within days of returning home from Athens I decided to enter my next marathon in Barcelona – less than five months later – and set myself the goal of running half an hour quicker. After another good build-up I started the race in Barcelona feeling really strong. I ran the first half in 1 hour and 46 minutes, on schedule for a finishing time of just under 3 hours and 35 minutes. In Barcelona I didn't have any friends running alongside me advising caution and in the following 10km I realised I was not running so effortlessly any more. Just short of the 18 mile point I was overtaken by a man holding a red balloon for the 3 hour 45 minute-pace group. From there to the end I really struggled, eventually reaching the finish in 4 hours and 1 minute. I had learned the lesson of good pace judgement, knowing that I had run the first half of the race too quickly.

KEY POINTS

- Reduce your training and allow adequate recovery in the final few weeks before the race
- Practise running at your intended marathon race pace – but in a controlled fashion and over relatively short distances
- Anticipate the feelings that you might have to deal with in running your marathon.

VIEW FROM THE ROAD
Mara Yamauchi: Getting ready for hot race conditions in Japan

British international marathon runner Mara Yamauchi finished 9th in the 2007 World Championship Marathon in Osaka

By the time my build up had started, I had been preparing for over a year for the conditions I would face in Osaka. I had begun to wear a tracksuit during training runs to get my body used to sweating more. This also got me into the habit of drinking more during and after training. I also tried to do some of my training during the warmer parts of the day, and in the two and a half weeks before the race I stayed in Tokyo to get used to the conditions. At the start of this period I trained around 4.30a.m. – the coolest part of the day – to allow my body to adjust to the hot weather. Then, as I gradually got used to the heat, I trained later in the day, although rarely after 9a.m., since the race start was at 7a.m. At home we deliberately did not use air conditioning until mid-afternoon. I also got into a routine of getting up at 3a.m. (the time I would have to get up on race day) and going to sleep at about 7p.m. I also practised drinking a lot in training, trying to estimate my sweat rate by measuring body weight before and after sessions. This helped me to decide how much I needed to drink on race day. In the race itself I managed to avoid severe dehydration and overheating – even though the temperatures got above 30 degrees. I was even able to run a negative split by a few seconds. If there was one mistake, it was trying to push the pace too soon (after 28km) – which meant that I faded a bit over the last 10km. Also in my eagerness to avoid dehydration I may have drunk too much during the race – getting the balance just right is quite difficult!

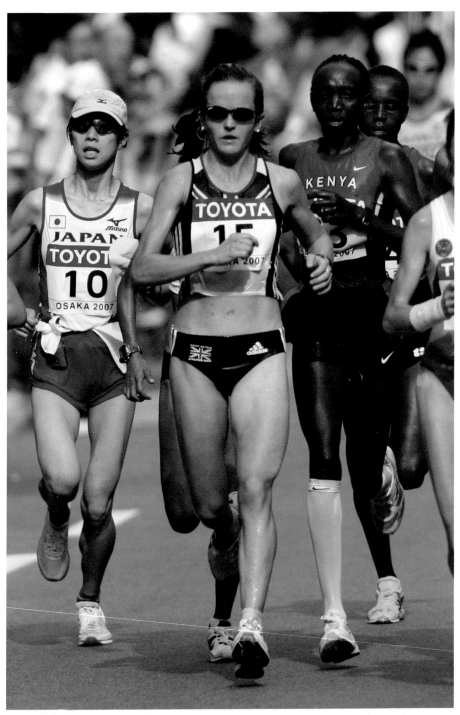

Mara Yamauchi (centre) in action in the 2007 IAAF World Championship Marathon in Osaka (see View from the Road on p. 101)

USEFUL TIPS
Planning a race strategy

Here are some tips for planning out your racing strategy:

- *Start slowly.* Even among experienced runners there is a mistaken view that you should get ahead of your schedule while you are feeling fresh, and then try not to slow down too much in the latter stages of the race. This strategy usually results in a dramatic slowdown in the second half of the race. Good performances are more often achieved either by level-pace running or by 'negative splits' – where the second half of the race is run faster than the first. The point is that if you blow up in a marathon, you can blow up badly and with a long way still to go. Conversely, if you're slightly behind schedule, yet still feeling good, you have plenty of time to catch up.

- *Break the distance down into sections.* The thought of having to cover 26 miles can be a daunting prospect for even the best-trained runner. You might find it easier to break the race down into segments – e.g. in 10km sections, or 10 miles/halfway/20 miles/finish – and concentrate on each stretch in turn. Reaching the end of each segment will also give you a chance to check your time and monitor your effort, and if need be adjust your pace or time goals.

- *Hold yourself back when you start to feel good.* Perhaps the best bit of advice I received before I ran my first marathon went something like this: 'If you're feeling good at 10 miles, restrain yourself from going any faster. If you're feeling good at halfway, still hold yourself back. If you're still feeling good at 16 miles, again hold back. At 20 miles you *will* feel tired, and then you can start racing'. The experience of many marathoners is that they hold themselves back early in the race, but then start to feel good at around halfway and run too quickly too soon, thinking that their good feeling will last all the way to the finish. Feelings can be deceptive, however: they then discover that the last six miles of the marathon last much longer than they could ever have imagined.

- *Start to focus after 16 miles.* The same advice as above, but more in terms of your mental focus. It's easy to focus on giving your best when you're feeling good, but not so easy when you're feeling tired. If you're well prepared, you should be able to cruise along for the first 10 or 12 miles of the marathon with time and energy to savour the atmosphere of the occasion. But as you do this, anticipate that it will get harder, and start to 'focus in' as the race enters its more trying moments and tiredness sets in.

- *Take advantage of running in a group.* Remember that you use up more energy when running at the front of a group. You may be able to control the pace that way, but others have the advantage of being shielded from either wind or air resistance. Running in a group also allows you to concentrate more on your rhythm rather than thinking specifically about how fast you are running. There may be times when it helps you to be at the front, but there will also be times when it is better for you to 'hide' in the group.

Race-day arrangements

A useful way to reduce pre-race anxiety is to ensure that you have made arrangements for your movements on the day of your marathon. The more obvious issues are:

- How will you get to the start?
- Where will you meet up with your friends and supporters after the race?
- How will you get home afterwards?

Nowadays, most organisers of big-city marathons (and the travel agencies who work with them) are highly efficient in putting on services to help runners with such arrangements. However, it is just as well that you find out for yourself what is going to happen. Try to be as specific as possible in the detail of these plans, remembering that many other runners will be on the move at the same time with precisely the same objective. On race day itself, you may be too nervous to think about anything else but running the race, and after the race you will almost certainly be too tired to do anything about it.

You should also be familiar with your race-day routine:

- You'll need to eat breakfast about three hours before the start of the marathon, which will mean eating at around 6.00–6.30a.m. – since many marathons start around 9.00a.m. In the week leading up to the race – or ideally, earlier in your preparation before one of your long runs – try out this routine. (For what you should eat, *see* Chapter 4, pp. 75–91.)
- You should have a clear idea of how you will warm up before the marathon. The most important thing is to stay warm before you start running. This might entail a few minutes of easy jogging followed by light stretching in the 15–20 minutes before the race begins. But you should do this without expending any unnecessary energy. The faster your starting speed, the longer you will require to complete an adequate warm-up.
- Immediately after the race, the most important thing is to stay warm, and to start replenishing your energy stores by drinking plenty and even eating small snacks. If possible it's better to walk for 10 minutes after you reach the finish than simply to collapse in a heap. Then aim to get into a hot bath as soon as is conveniently possible.

Your kit-bag for race day should include the following:

- *Your racing kit.* Make sure that you are comfortable with your racing gear by running in it at least once in training before the marathon. Pin your race number on your vest or T-shirt on the evening before the race. If you're unsure whether to wear a singlet or T-shirt in the race, wear both to the start and then decide.
- *Your racing shoes.* It's better not to race in an entirely new pair of shoes; you should try them out in training at least two or three times before the race, ideally in the course of one of your long runs. Bear in mind that your feet will expand slightly as the race goes on.
- *Toilet paper* – in case you run out of time to queue for the portaloos before the start of the race.
- *Vaseline* to smear on your toes/nipples/under your arms/between your thighs – or any part of you that is likely to chafe while running your marathon.
- *A plastic bin-liner* for a wet day, or *a woolly hat and gloves* for a cold day – all of which you can dispense with once the gun goes for the start of the race, or as soon as you are moving fast enough to generate heat.
- *A change of clothes for after the race* – even more important if it is likely to be wet.
- *A high-carbohydrate drink* which you can sip on the way to the start and as you stand on the start line (*see* also Chapter 4), and a small snack for after the race.

You can save yourself a lot of unnecessary worry and nervous energy on race day if you pay attention to these details before you actually go to the starting line. Good race performances, while never guaranteed, usually follow sound and thorough preparation.

Like many big-city marathons, the Brighton Marathon has a start time of 9am

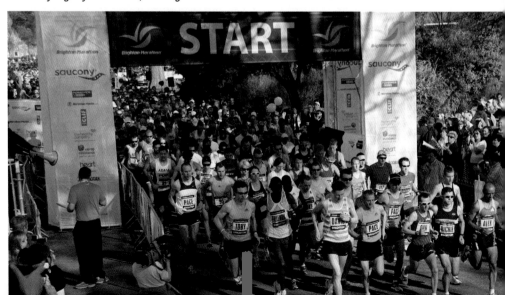

COUNTDOWN TO ATLANTA
ATLANTA, AUGUST 1996

Sixteen days before the 1996 Olympic Marathon, I flew from my training camp in Colorado to Atlanta, where Gail met me at the airport. She had conveniently arranged to do some research at Emory University in Atlanta for the duration of the Games, and was staying at an apartment in Virginia Highlands not far from the Olympic Village.

The evening of my arrival in Atlanta coincided with the Opening Ceremony in the new Olympic Stadium. However, I had decided to stay away from these festivities, which lasted long into the night. It was enough excitement just to experience the sultry heat of a summer's evening in Atlanta and to know that my competition was now not far away. The following afternoon I took a further 40-minute flight from Atlanta to join the British team at our holding camp in the northern Florida town of Tallahassee.

OLYMPIC HOLDING CAMP IN TALLAHASSEE

The purpose of the holding camp, on the campus of Florida State University, was to enable British athletes to acclimatise to the hot and humid conditions that we would encounter in Atlanta. The climate in Tallahassee turned out to be even more severe than in Atlanta: going out of the air-conditioned buildings felt – at least for the first few days – like walking into a sauna, with temperatures in the mid-thirties and humidity around 90 per cent.

In the course of the 12 days that I would be spending at the holding camp I had planned to do three hard sessions. I had already reduced my volume of training in the previous week to allow for the exertions involved in travelling. Staying fresh to perform well in my final few workouts was now of greater concern than maintaining a high overall volume of training. My final three workouts were designed primarily to get me used to the exertion of running hard in the heat. Bruce and Sue had joined me, and were able to offer their support during my sustained tempo runs on the dirt trails of the Tallahassee Forest Reserve. It was good to do these sessions out of the public eye, and away from the heat of the action. At this stage, I didn't need to prove my fitness to anybody – it was more a question of getting myself mentally prepared for performing on the big stage in Atlanta.

An outline of my taper for the race in Atlanta is shown in Table 5.3.

Staying in a training camp for the entire period of my taper meant that I had plenty of time to relax once training was over. Indeed, a great sense of anticipation prevailed over the camp as, both individually and as a team of British athletes, we prepared ourselves for competition. Each evening we

TABLE 5.3 TAPERING FOR THE OLYMPIC MARATHON (ATLANTA, 1996)

Days to go	Hard efforts	Total volume (km)
19	15km inc. 5 × (2km fast, 1km cruise)	3 weeks to go: 153km
16–14	Travel to Atlanta, then to Tallahassee	2 weeks to go: 160km
11	24km at good aerobic pace	—
8	10km at fast, increasing pace	—
5	16km at fast but relaxed pace	In week before marathon: 112km
3	Transfer back to Atlanta	—

would gather in the main living room in front of the large-screen TV to follow the progress of other team members who had already started competing. The long hours of waiting filled me both with excitement and apprehension. In the final week before competition my daily routine of training involved a couple of easy half-hour runs. The total weekly volume of training had been reduced from a maximum of around 240km in my hardest training period to 112km in the final week before competition. Now, all my steady running between the hard sessions was done at a relaxed pace. During these runs I would picture myself running on stretches of the course which I had visited three times over the past two years. To sharpen my focus for the race I spent a few sessions discussing possible race scenarios with the team psychologist. I also tried to anticipate the pre-race excitement I would encounter once I moved into the Olympic Village.

We had plenty of time to relax as the race drew near. To kill time and help switch off from thoughts of competition, we took a day trip to the Gulf Coast and had an afternoon at a local resort.

As the Games progressed, athletes started to leave Tallahassee and transfer to the Olympic Village in Atlanta in preparation for competition. Since I was competing on the final day, I was the last athlete to leave the camp. Fortunately, even until the day before I left, I continued to enjoy the support in Tallahassee of my coach, the medical officers and other members of the British Olympic team staff. Three days before my race I flew back to Atlanta and moved into the Olympic Village. The waiting was now almost over.

READY FOR THE 'OFF'

The 1996 Olympic Marathon took place on a warm, humid morning (26°C, 76 per cent humidity) in Atlanta on 4 August. The course consisted of a series of hills over the first 10 miles, a relatively flat middle section to 17 miles, a long gradual downhill for the next two miles, followed by three severe rises between 19 and 24 miles before finally dropping back to the finish in the stadium.

A week earlier, Fatima Roba of Ethiopia had won the women's marathon by holding the lead for the entire second half of the race. In the men's race things were likely to be different, since the competition at the front of the field was tighter. The tough nature of the course and the conditions also suggested that the outcome of the race would be left until the latter stages.

A few miles into the race, two Polish runners – Leszek Beblo and Grzegorz Gajdus – opened up a small lead. Though they were never more than 50m clear of the chasing group, they maintained their lead for the next 10km. At around the 10-mile point, as we turned onto Piedmont Avenue, the chasing pack drew level with the two Polish runners. The pace then slowed for the next few miles, enabling a large group of more than 25 runners to come back together as we passed the halfway mark in 1:07:40. Rounding a U-turn just short of 25km, the Brazilian Luiz dos Santos initiated a surge. I sensed that after such a slow middle part of the race – over the previous five miles the pace had dropped to 5:15 min/mile, or the equivalent of 2:18 pace – this move could be decisive, so I went with the leading group of five or six runners. But on the downhill section to 30km, the pace eased again and we were back to a leading group of about 18.

We now approached the series of hills starting at 19 miles. For the past two miles I had been struggling to ward off the feeling of needing to make a 'pit stop', yet knowing that at such a crucial part of the race I couldn't afford to stop.* Then, as we started the climb up the first hill, a break was made – and within half a mile the pack of 18 runners was spread out in single file up the road ahead of me.

---

*As well as ensuring that I started the race with high stores of glycogen – achieved through the normal process of carbo-loading in the three days before the race – I had also sought to guard against the effects of severe dehydration, a potential hazard in view of the hot race conditions we were likely to encounter. To this end, I drank a lot of fluid – a combination of water and weak concentrations of both isotonic and carbohydrate solutions – in the 48 hours before the race. Then on race-day morning, after an early breakfast at 3.30a.m. – the race began at 7.00a.m. – I consumed 1.5 litres of a glycerol drink about two hours before the start. (Glycerol aids water retention in the body, so can be particularly effective where the risk of severe dehydration exists.) Once the race was underway I continued to consume fluids at the drinks stations along the course (roughly 100–150ml every 5km). It is possible that after 90 minutes of running, my system was overloaded.

I tried to respond but was still bothered by the need to empty my system. Then, as I moved from 12th up to 10th by passing Dionisio Ceron and Steve Moneghetti, it all came out on the run! Up at the front, three runners – the South African Josiah Thugwane, the Korean Lee Bong-Ju and the Kenyan Eric Wainana – were contesting the lead. They held a gap of about 20 seconds over Martin Fiz in fourth. Behind them a chase was on for the minor positions.

Relieved of my earlier problems I fought my way back up the field, moving into sixth at the 36km point and passing the Mexican German Silva to go into fifth just short of 40km. As I entered the Olympic Stadium, the three medallists were entering the home straight. Thugwane took gold, Bong-Ju took silver and Wainana bronze, with Fiz finishing in fourth. I was fifth, 63 seconds behind the winner.

Unable to respond to the decisive move made by the leaders on the first series of hills, I had never got into a position to contest for a medal in the race's closing stages. I was disappointed not to win a medal. But the further I came away from the race, the more I could take comfort in the knowledge that I had peaked at just the right time. I also realised that the training I had done that year had been right for me at that particular stage of my career. I had trained at my limit and struck a good balance between speed and endurance. At times the training had seemed hard and unrelenting. That I had mastered the task so successfully was due to sound planning, total commitment and not a small dose of good fortune. With a fifth-place finish at the Olympics I knew it had been well worth it.

Passing the 25-mile point in fifth place in the 1996 Olympic Marathon

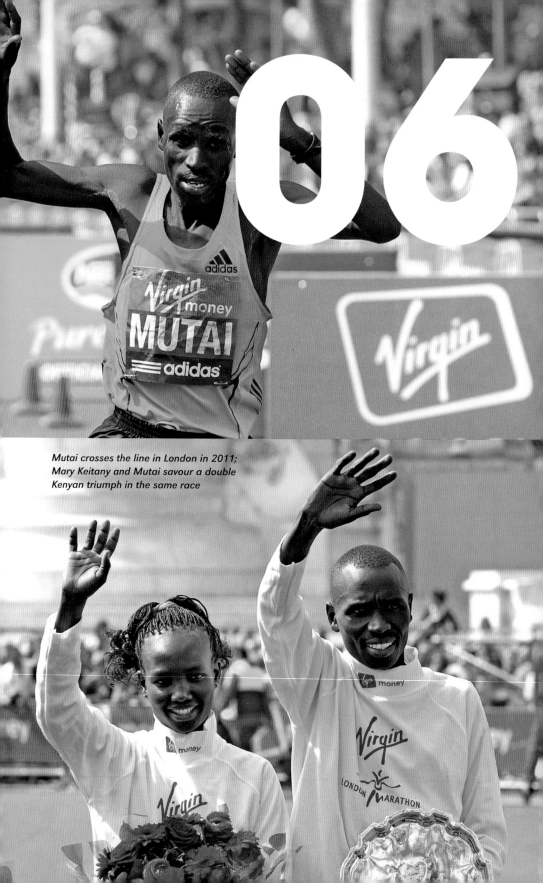

06

*Mutai crosses the line in London in 2011;
Mary Keitany and Mutai savour a double
Kenyan triumph in the same race*

THE RACE EXPERIENCE

PEAK PERFORMANCE

What is it that makes some runners race better than they train? Or conversely, why do some runners who put so much effort into their training have so little to show for it when it comes to racing? Your race experience can be quite different from anything you have encountered in training. It's not simply a question of how much effort is involved – indeed, there may be times when you feel that you have to work harder in training than in your races. It has more to do with the mental demands imposed upon you by the race situation.

- **How will you cope with your surges of nervous energy?**
- **Will you be able to exploit the excitement created by the crowds of spectators around you?**
- **Will you channel your competitive instincts, or let them get the better of you?**

If you are able to master these aspects of the race experience, you are more likely to get the best out of yourself once the competition has begun.

In Chapter 5 (pp. 106–109), I gave an account of how Josiah Thugwane became the first black South African ever to win the Olympic Marathon. Thugwane was relatively unknown in the world of marathon running going into the 1996 Olympic Games. Expectations about South African runners performing well in the event lay with his better-known compatriots, Gert Thys and Lawrence Peu, who had already made a name for themselves on the US road-racing circuit. So how was it that Thugwane was able to produce such a stunning run in Atlanta? Firstly, no doubt, because his training had brought him to a peak of physical fitness on race day; secondly, and as importantly, because he had reserved his best for the race. In his training sessions with

VIEW FROM THE ROAD
Vince Grealy: Great experience, but hard work

Vince Grealy broke 4 hours for his first marathon in London
My experience of doing the marathon was amazing. The sense of being part of such a big event, the atmosphere and especially the crowd support was quite remarkable. It is something every runner should experience. I still get butterflies just thinking about it. Having said that, the pain was worse than I expected, even though it was not my first marathon. Maybe because I was fitter I was expecting more from myself, and did not get that in terms of my finishing time. Race day was also much hotter than I expected and I got a little sunburnt. One thing I could not have anticipated, since it had never happened on any of my long training runs, was that my watch rubbed a deep bruise in my wrist in the second half of the race, perhaps due to the extra salt from sweating so much.

Thys and Peu in Albuquerque in the run-up to the Games he had been happy to play the role of the follower. By winning in Atlanta, Thugwane showed that he knew best how to race, and to race at his very best when it mattered most.

> **'By winning in Atlanta, Thugwane showed that he knew best how to race, and to race at his very best when it mattered most.'**

In this chapter I examine three aspects of the race experience that can influence performance:

- adrenaline and excitement
- crowds
- commitment.

ADRENALINE AND EXCITEMENT
Amy's story
One year to the day after watching her first marathon, here was Amy – yes, couch-potato, feet-up-on-the-couch-with-a-drink Amy – actually running her first one! As she awoke on race-day morning, the butterflies that hadn't left her stomach all week now seemed more active than ever. Her running friend

guru had told her that it was better to head to the start line with a feeling of dread than one of complacency. So in this respect at least, she comforted herself that her last-minute preparations were going to plan.

Arriving at the start of the race two hours later, she found herself wrestling with a quite different, yet equally overpowering, sensation. As she began to notice thousands of other runners converging on the start area, and what seemed like even larger numbers of spectators lining the opening stretch of the marathon route, it suddenly dawned on her that today wasn't only her big moment – it was the big moment, the culmination of weeks and months of preparation and anticipation for thousands of other runners and running supporters. She would need to rely solely on her own individual effort to cover the 26 miles ahead of her, but this would happen alongside masses of other runners doing precisely the same thing.

For a brief moment, Amy wished that she could savour – for longer than the 30 minutes that remained before the starting gun would fire – this wonderful feeling of carnival. She was quickly brought back to reality as another flutter of fear danced across her stomach. No, she couldn't wait a moment longer for the race to begin.

The roadside digital clock showed 56 minutes and three seconds as Amy cruised past the 10km marker. She could hardly believe it: after days of dreading the pain of running a marathon, those opening miles had felt so easy. Amy could almost have admitted to having enjoyed running them! Seeing a group of friends cheering and waving excitedly at her four miles into the race had given her a boost, and now – almost four minutes ahead of her schedule – she began to consider abandoning her pre-race plans and concentrating simply on keeping up with the runners around her. After all, she could hardly hear herself breathing so, she figured, she still had bags of energy in reserve.

Three hours into the race, her friends had regrouped at the 30km mark. Anxiously waiting for a glimpse of Amy coming around the corner, they sensed that she might be in a spot of trouble. Another half-hour later, a weary-looking Amy came into sight, prompting one of her friends to issue a cry as much of relief as encouragement. This time, Amy did not have the means to respond. Her early surge of enthusiasm had evaporated soon after she reached the 10-mile marker, and for the past 30 minutes of her journey she had felt as if she were running 'on empty'. And there was still a long way to go to the finish. Carried away by the occasion, she had abandoned all her careful planning – and her big moment had crashed.

Recognising the different ways in which you react to a training and a race situation can help you to perform at your best when it most matters. Some aspects of your race performance – for instance, running efficiently and to a set speed over an extended period – can be practised in training; while others

– such as the heightened intensity of nerves before a race and of effort during competition – can be anticipated, but are harder to rehearse.

I learned this lesson the hard way at the time of the 1996 Olympic Marathon (an account of which is given on pp. 106–109 of Chapter 5). In the three months of training leading up to the race I regularly rehearsed the eating and drinking routine that I planned to use for the marathon itself. Despite this, I still encountered problems in the race itself. (For more on the unpredictable elements of competition, *see* Chapter 11.)

Mindful of the way in which your pre-race nerves might affect you, you should sort out many of the practical details for running your marathon in advance of race day (see also pp. 104–105). Allow too for the likelihood that on race-day morning, your stomach will be churning more than usual. This might involve bringing forward the time of your pre-race breakfast snack: whereas in the course of normal training you might get away with having breakfast just two hours before setting out on a long run, on the morning before you run your marathon you may need to allow a little longer for your food to digest.

As well as understanding how your state of apprehension might hinder performance, you should also recognise ways in which it can enhance it. When I line up at the start of a race, there is always something that makes me want to fight harder and dig deeper than I am ever able to do in training. Maybe it's because I know that there's nowhere to hide in competition. The race will betray my true level of fitness – I have to 'produce the goods' here. I can still remember that empty feeling as a schoolboy, nervous before some of my earliest cross-country races. Would I be fast enough to get up to the front? Would I be able to hang on when my rivals made a surge? I also used to dread the thought that my laces would snap as I was tying up my shoes before the start (which they sometimes did). Those pre-race nerves felt pretty awful at the time, but no doubt they helped me to run well once the race got underway.

Have you ever tried doing a time trial in training? I sometimes choose to run a time trial in preference to a race, because I know that it won't draw on my competitive instincts to the same degree. I want to store up those resources for when it really matters. Although it often feels as if I'm pushing myself as hard in a time trial as in a race, my times in the time trial never come out as fast as in the proper race. Why? Because in time trials I am short of that adrenaline-producing excitement of the race that helps to counteract feelings of tiredness and pain.

Three weeks before competing in the 1997 London Marathon I ran a tough 30km time trial on the quiet country roads around my former home in Marlborough, covering the distance in 1:32:18. When it came to the race itself, I ran the first 30km in 1:30:52 and then kept going for a further 12km at roughly the same pace. The whole atmosphere of the race occasion spurred me on to greater levels of performance.

Staying in control

If you watch small children running fast, rarely is there a sense of them holding anything in reserve. It is all or nothing; what counts is the present; the finish line is never far away. But while the excitement of young children is unchecked and immediate, the excitement experienced by marathon runners has to be controlled and spread over a long period. If it is not, and too much child-like aggression is shown in the early stages of a race, the runner will soon come to grief. By contrast, the runner who can keep these feelings of aggression under wraps until a point in the race when they are most needed is more likely to be successful at the marathon.

Some years before I ran my first marathon, I remember watching Gelindo Bordin race to victory in the 1990 Boston Marathon. Bordin knew a thing or two about the art of controlled aggression, having come from behind in the final two miles to win the 1988 Olympic Marathon two years earlier. Bordin's Olympic victory had demonstrated the importance of keeping something in reserve for the latter stages of a marathon. The toughest part of the Boston Marathon course is the stretch of road known as 'Heartbreak Hill' – a series of long gradual rises between 17 and 21 miles. Bordin knew he would have to make his main effort at this point in the race if he were to have any chance of winning. He was content therefore to run some way behind the leading group of Africans in the race's early stages. After 16 miles he was still only in sixth place, almost a minute behind the leaders. As they approached the hills, Bordin started to make his move. By 18 miles he had moved into third, with the gap to the leader, Juma Ikangaa, reduced to 49 seconds. At 20

Q&A WHAT IS MEANT BY 'RUNNING ETIQUETTE'?

Even at the highest levels of competition complaints are sometimes made of athletes clipping the heels of their competitors or using their elbows excessively to get past other runners. 'Running etiquette' is in effect the unwritten rules about how runners should pay attention to fellow participants and applies to all levels of competition. It may involve thinking of where to stand at the start of the race, or how to pass other runners, or where to stop if you have to stop in mid-race. Similarly, when running in a group it may involve taking your turn in pacing others around you, so that you are not 'drafting' for the entire distance. In the end, etiquette comes down to realising that you and your result are not the only things that matter in a competition.

miles he was in second, 16 seconds behind Ikangaa. On the final section of Heartbreak Hill, running on the other side of the road to Ikangaa, Bordin swept into the lead.

From that point on, no one doubted that Bordin would end up the winner. (In fact, he went on to win by a huge 93-second margin.) The six Africans who had set the early pace had run the first half of the race in the bewilderingly fast time of 1:02:01. To keep the leaders in his sights – albeit 300m down the road – Bordin had had to run faster than cool rationale would have suggested. He had covered the first half of the course in 1:02:46. But in refusing to get caught up in the excitement of the race's early stages, and holding back his biggest effort for when it really mattered, Bordin skilfully outplayed and outran his opposition.

CROWDS

My first ever race in the Olympic arena was an unforgettable experience. What made it particularly memorable were the crowds at the Olympic Stadium in Barcelona on that warm summer evening in late July 1992.

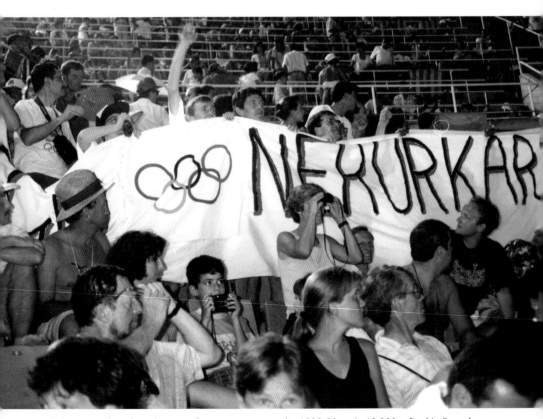

Being seen, if not heard: some of my supporters at the 1992 Olympic 10,000m final in Barcelona

We were being called to the start of the first heat of the 10,000m. A first-eight finish in the heat ensured a place in the final three days later. A few hours earlier, the capacity crowd in the Mont Juig Olympic Stadium had seen their home favourite from Barcelona, Daniel Plaza, win the first gold medal of track and field competition in the 20km walk. Moments after the gun was fired for the start of our race came an announcement in the stadium that the medal ceremony for Plaza's – and Spain's first – gold medal was being postponed until the following evening. The crowd went hysterical in being denied what they had waited all evening for. They started whistling incessantly and waving white handkerchiefs (as a sign of disapproval) – imitating the worst antics of Barcelona's soccer fans. We ran our heat oblivious to the reasons for their hysteria, but could hardly remain unaffected by the excitement generated by the crowds. I ended up finishing third in the race, thus qualifying for the Olympic 10,000m final. Three days later the atmosphere in the stadium was equally charged as 20 of us – Ethiopian against Kenyan, Spaniard against Moroccan, American against Mexican – lined up for the final where I ended up finishing a disappointing 17th.

Crowds can and do affect your performance. They can inspire you or conspire against you – or both, as I discovered when running the London Marathon in 1997 (*see* below). They can reassure you, or unsettle you. They can urge you on to an even greater show of effort, or they can make your pace judgement go completely haywire. But one thing is for certain. They won't go away, so it's good to learn to live with them.

COMMITMENT

Getting the best out of yourself on race day also depends to a large extent on your desire to perform well. If something is really important to you, you will be prepared to put yourself out to make it happen.

I remember once meeting a former Soviet swimming coach from the old communist system who had taken a new job working with the Austrian national swimming team. He complained that though the Austrian swimmers had ability and trained well, they lacked the real desire to succeed. In Russia, he recalled, athletes not only wanted to win, but *needed* to win. It was a matter of priorities.

I have often found that my best performances come after a period of sustained hard training. I know how hard I've worked to reach my level of fitness. I'm desperately keen to demonstrate my true level of fitness. It has become a question of necessity that I turn my fitness into results.

> **'You should train not simply to get into great shape,
> but to get into great shape for a specific race on
> a specific day – and then give all of your best.
> That's what peak performance is all about.'**

EXPERT COMMENT
Liz McColgan: Giving it your all

Liz McColgan won the 1996 London Marathon and was Britain's best female distance runner of the 1990s

On race-day morning, my thoughts were always on preparing myself to run the hardest race of my life. I would always think the worst, which meant that I would be prepared for any eventuality during the race.

My theory for running a good marathon was to run the first half feeling as comfortable as possible. My focus was on staying relaxed and then thinking about increasing my effort over the second half. It turned out that most of my races were negative splits.

On the day before the 1997 London Marathon, I fell over when crossing the road but didn't let it bother me too much. The next day, once the race started I got severe stomach pains, which I thought were caused by drinking too much so I stopped taking drinks at the feed stations. But the pain didn't go away. After 22 miles I was still in a lot of pain, was only in fifth place and was about to drop out. Then we passed a huge crowd of people standing under Tower Bridge. The noise was deafening, so much so that it lifted my spirits and I began to stop worrying about how I was feeling and began to race again. Within the next few miles I had got back into the lead, only to be beaten by Joyce Chepchumba in a sprint finish. It was one of the hardest races that I had ever run. The next day I discovered that the stomach pain was due to a torn muscle from my fall before the race. It was amazing to think how the crowds had helped me that day.

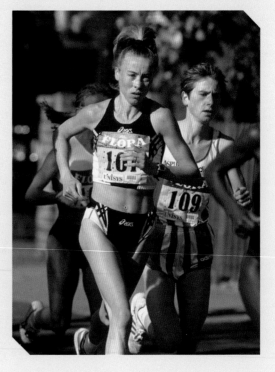

Liz McColgan in action in the 1997 London Marathon

VIEW FROM THE ROAD
John Feeney: 'Hitting the wall' in Prague

John Feeney suffers in the heat in Prague

My decision to run the Prague Marathon was prompted by my failure to obtain a place in the London Marathon. I had been suffering from shin splints throughout the winter which really disrupted and delayed my training plan. During this time, I decided to buy a bicycle to ensure that I maintained cardiovascular fitness and muscle strength. However, I was able to resume training in March and felt confident to run the Bath Half-Marathon in March. Successfully completing the half-marathon gave me the confidence to increase my training preparation for Prague. After six weeks, I was able to complete three long runs of between 18 and 20 miles. In addition, I did one medium-long run of 8–10 miles and a speed session each week. I was also cycling twice a week which provided a degree of variety as well as aiding my overall fitness.

By the time the marathon arrived, I felt strong and confident that I would meet my target time of 3 hours 50 minutes. My aim was to run the first 20 miles in about 2 hours 50 minutes, leaving the remaining six miles or so to be run at a nice steady pace. Race day was very warm. While I managed to stick to my pace, the heat began to take effect after about 13 miles. The heat was being radiated from the road surface, making it seem warmer than it actually was. I found myself taking on additional water and began to doubt whether I would be able to finish – I guess I hit the so-called 'wall' earlier than I had ever done before. I found myself spending slightly longer at each water station and reached the 20-mile mark just outside my target time.

The remaining six miles seemed to take an eternity. My efforts over the previous 20 miles left me absolutely drained. I eventually reached the finish line in 4 hours 19 minutes, some 30 minutes slower than anticipated but at least 12 minutes faster than my previous run in London. After the marathon, although my legs didn't feel too tired, I was surprised by the effect the heat had on me. If I was running in that type of heat again, I would slow down my running pace and take on small amounts of fluids at regular intervals rather than gulping down water at each water station.

My coach Bruce had a similar approach in his competitive days. In his races he would expend so much effort in his attempt to drive himself harder towards the finish that he was often physically sick when he got there. The race situation was an intense experience, demanding from the athlete total commitment of effort and resolve.

If you are serious about trying to peak for performance, at whatever level you may be competing, you should try to focus all your efforts on the one task ahead of you. The nearer you get to the race, the narrower your focus becomes. You will need not only to train specifically for the event, but also to think clearly about how you plan to run the race. You should train not simply to get into great shape, but to get into great shape for a specific race on a specific day – and then give all of your best. That's what peak performance is all about.

KEY POINTS
- Expect to feel nervous before a competition, and develop ways of channelling this energy towards higher levels of performance
- Try to take advantage of the excitement created by the race experience
- Learn to reserve your biggest effort for the latter stages of your marathon
- Resolve to give all of your best: commitment is everything.

USEFUL TIPS
Anticipating problems on race day
Assuming that you have trained well, that you have worked out a good race strategy (*see* pp. 103–104), and that you have made thorough pre-race arrangements (*see* pp. 104–105), you should feel confident about achieving your goal as you go to the start of the marathon. However, the true nature of the challenge before you is only just beginning as you actually set about running the race.

How should you anticipate possible dangers along the way?

- *Crowds of participating runners.* You may find that the pace at which you start your marathon is determined by the pace of the runners around you, rather than by your own planned schedule. Don't panic if this happens. Remember that it's much easier to catch up on your schedule if you've started too slowly than to maintain your pace if you've gone out too quickly. You may have done many of your long training runs on your own, but come race day you may find yourself surrounded by a sea of runners for most of the distance. If you can't physically practise what this will feel like, try to imagine yourself in this situation so that it comes as less of a shock on the day of your marathon.

- *Crowds on the course.* Let them be an encouragement to you, but not to the extent that they make you run too fast too soon. Many runners tell the story of getting carried away by the excitement of the occasion, running ahead of their pre-race schedules and paying for it at the end (*see* 'Amy's story', p. 112–114).
- *Highs and lows of the race.* No matter how well you perform, you're likely to experience at least a few dark moments in the race. It may be something physical (such as a stomach problem or a painful blister – *see* below), or simply a feeling of doubt about achieving your goal. It may help to anticipate how you might react in such situations and to develop your own mechanisms for coping with such problems.
- *Being unable to take drinks at the drinks stations* (due perhaps to overcrowding, or a shortage of drinks). Though this is unlikely to occur, you may need to think quickly: ask to share a fellow runner's drink or else wait until the next water station. (In some marathons, drinks stations offering water and sponges are placed midway between stations offering special glucose drinks.)
- *Physical problems.* Many of these hazards can be eliminated in the course of training (which will have given you experience of addressing such problems). You should be comfortable in your racing shoes and in your racing gear; you should know when and how much to drink; you might even have had to put up with cramp or a sidestitch in training. Use this experience, and the knowledge that you have endured worse things in training, to help you either avoid or put up with such problems if they do occur in your marathon.
- *'Hitting the wall'.* Technically, the term refers to the act of slowing down dramatically once your glycogen reserves have been exhausted (*see* also pp. 76–82). Once you reach this state, you have to rely exclusively on fat as a source of fuel. This will allow you to keep going but – because of its less efficient work-rate as discussed in Chapter 4 – you will be forced to slow down. There are ways, however, in which you can reduce the likelihood of this happening. The most obvious way in training is by doing long runs which get your body used to drawing on both fat *and* glycogen as a source of fuel – thus conserving those vital glycogen stores for the latter stages of your marathon. (Some runners take this practice to the extreme by doing their long training runs on an empty stomach, believing that when already short of glycogen, the body will become even more efficient at conserving these limited reserves.) The dietary precautions necessary

to avoid 'hitting the wall' are outlined in Chapter 4. Note also that the term 'hitting the wall' is used by many marathon runners more broadly to describe a state of extreme fatigue – whether or not it results in a sudden reduction in running speed. In such a situation, how will you cope? Your energy and adrenaline will be running low. You may experience tiredness either in the form of a cramping sensation or as a feeling of 'heavy legs'. Willpower and determination may be your only hope of getting you to the finish.

VIEW FROM THE ROAD
Martin Stevens: making the most of experience

Martin Stevens took advantage of his knowledge of the London Marathon course

In April 2011 I ran my 11th London Marathon. My build-up was less than perfect. In fact I averaged less than 30 miles/week in the 11 weeks leading up to the race because of a back injury from the Marrakesh Marathon three months previously, although my last five weeks did include three long runs of over 20 miles. I set myself the goal of breaking 3 hours, hoping to run each 5km in around 21 minutes and giving me 12 minutes to run the last 2.2km. I ran the first 5km (which in London is slightly downhill) in 20:33 and from then on kept as even a pace as possible doing 5km splits of between 20:49 and 21:08.

Knowing the course really helped (I had run my PB of 2:44 in London two years previously), as did the support from my girlfriend and many of my club-mates who were marshalling between miles 16 and 18. I had a really bad patch after mile 19. I was just trying to count off the minutes until we got back onto The Highway. My 5km split to 35km was 21:26, my slowest so far. I dug in. The crowds on The Highway and along the Embankment picked me up. I reached 40km in 2:47:44 with a 5km split of 20:52, knowing that my sub-three hour goal was in sight. I enjoyed the last mile through Parliament Square and towards Buckingham Palace: it wasn't my fastest time, but it was just as satisfying achieving my time goal in tough circumstances.

EXPERT COMMENT Haile Gebrselassie: In at the deep end: my first international marathon

In 1988 a 15 year old Haile Gebrselasssie ran his first marathon in Addis Ababa, finishing in a time of 2:47. Fourteen years later, after winning two Olympic titles and four world titles over 10,000m, he returned to the marathon, with a third place finish in London in a time of 2:06:35

I trained really hard and with no major problems for my first international marathon in London in 2002 and I knew I was in great shape going into the race. I also knew that this was my first serious attempt at the distance and that the elite field, which included Khannouchi, Tergat and El Mouaziz, was really competitive.

On the morning of the race, I had my breakfast at six, more than three hours before the start, and at quarter past seven took the athletes' bus from the hotel to the start. Before the start, I was thinking about how I would follow the pacemakers, and was also trying to think what I would do if I had any bad feelings during the race. Even though I had done all the right training, as it was my first marathon I even wondered if I would finish the race and how the weather might affect me – London is quite different from Addis Ababa!

Once the race got underway, I kept listening to my body. I was also watching to see who was there running with us in the lead group, and thinking when I would next take water at the drink stations. The atmosphere was incredible. It seemed as if the crowd was shouting us on all the way around, and in places like the Cutty Sark and Tower Bridge they made so much noise that it lifted me for quite a few minutes after we had passed there.

My only bad patch came right at the end of the race. After running over the cobbles at 22 miles, I started to feel some tiredness in my legs, and then at 25 miles I really started to struggle. But I suppose that's what makes the marathon so hard. I was better prepared for my next race.

Haile Gebrselassie in his debut marathon in London in 2002 where Khalid Khannouchi ran a new world record of 2:05:38

TEN TIPS FOR THE ROAD

Advice from first-time marathon runners on getting the most out of your race experience:

1) Don't worry if the crowds of runners around you prevent you from running at your set pace for the first few miles of the marathon – there's plenty of tarmac ahead for you to make up the lost time.
2) If you need a leak during the marathon, try one of the pubs en route rather than queuing for a portaloo. You may find yourself waiting longer than you expected.
3) Prepare yourself for that feeling at 15 miles that it still seems a long way to the finish. The feeling is quite different from what you may have had at 15 miles on a 20-mile training run.
4) Suck glucose tablets or boiled sweets in the second half of your marathon to prevent your blood sugar levels from dropping too low.
5) Write your name on your vest if you want ten times more vocal support than your competitors.
6) Tell your friends which side of the road you will be running on at certain points en route – it will make it easier for them to spot you.
7) If you think you're going to 'hit the wall', you probably will. Stay positive, knowing that tiredness is a certain part of every marathoner's experience – but it need not defeat you.
8) After you finish, don't sit down for too long until you know you are somewhere where you won't have to move for quite a while.
9) If you stop for a celebratory drink, make sure the pub has a downstairs toilet – you may not make it upstairs in time.
10) Remember to enjoy the occasion.

The 1995 World Championship Marathon started at 3p.m. in temperatures over 30°C. Drinking and trying to keep cool in the early part of the race were essential

ON A HIGH FOR THE LONDON MARATHON
LONDON, APRIL 1997

In the days leading up to my debut appearance in the London Marathon I felt a great sense of anticipation about what I could achieve. The race organisers were keen to have a British winner in the men's race, following three consecutive victories by the Mexican Dionisio Ceron. This year Ceron would not be taking part in the London race, and much of the pre-race 'hype' centred on the confrontation between myself and Paul Evans, who two months after my fifth-place finish in Atlanta had won the Chicago Marathon in a time of 2:08:52.

A strong international field had also been assembled. Thugwane, the 1996 Olympic Marathon champion, would be running, but there was some doubt as to whether he could reproduce his Atlanta form. Antonio Pinto, the 1992 London Marathon winner, was coming back to one of his favourite race venues. He had already run four 2:08 marathons, although in my favour was the fact that I had beaten him in all three championship marathons that we had contested. Likewise Steve Moneghetti, the 1994 Commonwealth champion, had four 2:08 clockings to his credit, but I had beaten him in our two most recent encounters, in Gothenburg and Atlanta. Stefano Baldini, the 1996 World Half-Marathon champion, was also in the field, but he was still a relative novice at the full 26-mile distance, with a personal best of 2:11:01. This was a race I felt I could definitely win – if I could produce my best on the day.

RACE DAY IN LONDON

Race day brought with it near-perfect conditions for marathon running: blue skies and sunshine, and a temperature of around 10 degrees Celsius. As I looked out of our hotel window, the flags on Tower Bridge were hardly fluttering – a sign that the westerly wind that so often buffets the runners on the final four miles of the course might today be a less important factor. We had a light breakfast at 6.00a.m., were on the bus to the course at 7.15a.m., and arrived at the Elite Athlete tents near the start a little before 8.00a.m. An hour and a half later we were on the start line and ready to race.

Over the preceding eight years of my international career I had had some memorable racing moments. I will never forget, for instance, the experience of racing at the Bislett Games in Oslo, where the excitement of the occasion was heightened by the physical closeness of enthusiastic spectators filling the stadium to capacity. I have a vivid recollection, too, of another race in Norway when I first ran for Britain in the World Cross-Country Championships in Stavangar in 1989. There, the chant of cheering spectators for the entire 12km of the race was reminiscent of the incessant 'hop-hop-hop' cries heard in downhill slalom.

The feeling here on Blackheath Common at the start of the 1997 London Marathon was equally special. There was a sense that everything had come together well for this day. I was healthy and I was in great shape. The months of hard training and the years of waiting to run in this race were over. This was the day to perform. Out on the course ahead of me were thousands of enthusiastic spectators – not to mention the millions watching on television – who would be willing me on towards the finish. As soon as the race got underway, I tried to find a comfortable rhythm and stay relaxed, aiming to preserve as much energy as possible for the latter stages of the race. During the early miles I was aware of the shouts of encouragement from spectators along the route. Every other shout seemed to be for Eamonn Martin (the 1993 winner), who was up in the leading group for the first five miles, but there was still a lot of support for Paul and myself. Just before reaching the Cutty Sark in Greenwich, we went through 10km in 29:55, inside world-record schedule (which then stood at 2:06:50). The appointed pacemakers for the race were two Portuguese runners, Carlos Patricio and Paulo Catarino. They also had the same manager as a number of the leading runners in the field, including the two South Africans Thugwane and Peu and, more significantly, the Portuguese

THE WEATHER

The ideal conditions for running a marathon are a cool, dry and still day with temperatures in the range of 7–12 degrees Celsius. If it is too warm, you are more likely to encounter problems with dehydration; if it is too cold, your body might need to work harder to run at the required speed. Wind is more a hindrance than a help, because any gains made from running with a tailwind are outweighed by the additional effort needed in having to battle into a headwind. (The same can also be said of the respective ease and severity of running downhill and uphill on an undulating course.)

If you have to run your marathon on a cold day, you should consider starting the race wearing a hat and gloves – which can easily be discarded during the race. If it is too warm, you need to drink greater amounts of fluid both before and during the race. If it is windy, the best advice is to run in a group and take shelter from other runners – but also be prepared to take your share of the lead at certain stages in the race.

Q&A HOW CAN I PREPARE FOR HOT CONDITIONS?
This aspect of race preparation seems to be neglected time and again even at the highest level of performance – just witness the results of the Ethiopian team in the 2007 World Cross-Country Championships in Mombasa and, by contrast, the success of athletes such as 2007 world cross-country champion Lornah Kiplagat who prepare properly for extreme conditions. After spending two weeks in the humidity of San Juan in February 2007, for example, Kiplagat scored a convincing 10km road-race victory over Olympic 5000m champion Meseret Defar, who had arrived just a few days before the race. Mara Yamauchi's preparation for the 2007 World Championship Marathon in Osaka also provides some useful lessons about preparing to run in heat – see *View from the Road* on p. 101.

Pinto. Before the race, there had been some discussion among the runners and race organisers about the time that the pacemakers should aim for at half-distance. I had asked for between 1:03:45 and 1:04:00, while Pinto had requested between 1:03:15 and 1:03:30. Not surprisingly, Pinto's preference won out since it would be 'his' pacemakers who would be doing the running.

The early pace was maintained as we passed through Surrey Docks at nine miles. The leading group was now down to about 10 runners, in file formation: at the front were the two pacemakers, Patricio and Catarino; Pinto followed close behind; then came Evans and myself, Thugwane, his compatriot Lawrence Peu, Moneghetti, the German Stephane Franke and the Spaniard José Garcia. I was still feeling very good, and trying to retain a sense of running well within my capabilities.

THE CROWDS GO CRAZY
As we crossed Tower Bridge at 12½ miles, it felt as if we were hit by a blast of exuberant cheering from spectators on both sides of the road. We were still trying to keep our nervous energy under wraps – though the same could not be said of the crowds. They were going wild with excitement, and for a stretch of about 400m before we came off the far side of the bridge we were swept along by a wave of encouragement. This was more powerful than anything I had encountered in previous marathons, even including my recent Olympic experience.

We reached halfway in 1:03:28, at which point one of the pacemakers, Catarino, dropped out of the race. The other pacemaker, Patricio, stayed in the race for a further two miles, ensuring that the pace was maintained up to 15 miles (reached in 1:12:45). The leading group was now down to eight runners.

As Patricio stepped off the road, I found myself at the front of the field. I then made an error of judgement. Instead of letting another runner set the pace by dropping back to run with the group, I got caught up in the excitement of the occasion and continued to run at the front. After Patricio dropped out, I actually increased the pace from 4:56 for the 15th mile to 4:51 for the 16th mile (which also includes a slight uphill section approaching Canary Wharf). I was feeling strong and in charge of the race and started to sense the crowds urging me on to run even faster.

But this strategy was playing into the hands of my opponents, many of whom – like me – still felt full of running. By frontrunning I was simply acting as a pacemaker for the other runners, who were still keeping something in reserve for the latter stages. By contrast, I was using up unnecessary energy too early in the race.

After running for about seven or eight minutes out in front, I realised my mistake and dropped back to run level with the group. The pace then slowed over the next 5km. We reached 30km in a time of 1:30:52 (still on schedule to finish in 2:07:50). I was still feeling comfortable – though after 20 miles of fast running my feelings were perhaps not the best measure of exactly how much energy was still left in the tank.

At this point in the race, a leading group of eight (Pinto, Evans, Thugwane, Peu, Moneghetti, Garcia, the Kenyan Eric Kimaiyo and myself) had been joined by the Italian Baldini. Baldini had run a more prudent first part of the race, going through halfway in 1:04:15, some 45 seconds behind the leaders. Soon after he caught up with us he put in a surge to test out how we were all feeling. Thugwane and Kimaiyo went after him; Evans and I followed – though now we were both operating at close to our limit. We regrouped at 32km and ran together for a further three kilometres. At 35km Baldini put in another, more sustained surge, which again took Thugwane and Kimaiyo with him. The leading group was now down to three, I was in fourth some 20m behind, and Evans was a further 20m back.

This was a critical moment in the race. I knew that if I didn't keep up with the leaders now, my hopes of winning the race would be over. I dug deeper into my reserves and over the next kilometre clawed my way back to the leaders as we approached the cobbled stretch through the Tower of London. By this stage I was doing all I could just to stay up with them. As they maintained their pace over the cobbles, I again fell off the lead.

SURVIVAL

With three miles of the race to go, and the feeling that I was using every last drop of energy just to maintain my pace, I now entered the marathon runner's equivalent of the Death Zone, a mountaineering term for the stretch of the climb above 26,000 feet. I became less aware of my competitors, and even less so of the wildly cheering spectators along the Embankment. I had one focus, and one focus alone: holding everything together to reach the finish line in the shortest possible time. Now it was about survival. If I had had the presence of mind, I could have told myself that all those weeks of training in Tirrenia – the long runs, the punishing 25km tempo runs, the speed workouts – had not been done for nothing. But this wasn't the time to think rationally. It was more about raw determination. I survived those last few miles simply because I owed it to myself to survive them.

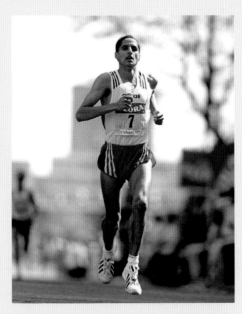

Surviving the last few miles in the 1997 London Marathon

The eventual race winner, Pinto, came storming past me just before I reached 25 miles. He went on to catch the leading trio, and then to out-sprint Baldini over the final 400m of the race. His winning time was a new course record of 2:07:55. I finished fifth in 2:08:36. This at least gave me the satisfaction of running 1½ minutes faster than I had ever run before for the marathon, and my new best time was the third-fastest ever by a British runner. Still, I couldn't hide my disappointment. I knew I had tried hard, that I had performed well, and that I had achieved my time goal. But I was also aware that I had failed in my quest to win the race. I had allowed the excitement and expectation of the occasion to cloud my judgement at a key stage in the competition. Had I the chance to run again, I would have done so differently: this had not been my perfect race. Racing, however, is not about what might have happened – it's about what actually does.

RUNNING THE SUB-TWO HOUR MARATHON

Records are there to be broken: marathon running's 'Bannister' moment – breaking 2 hours – will surely happen one day. The real question is when it will happen and what kind of athlete will achieve it.

One way of predicting how soon this barrier will be broken is by extrapolating from previous improvements on the record. Patrick Makau's 2011 world record of 2:03:38 was 21 seconds faster than Haile Gebrselassie's 2008 world record, itself a 99-second improvement on Khalid Khannouchi's 2002 record and more than eight minutes faster than Abebe Bekila's 1964 world record of 2:12:11. Depending on which comparisons are used, we could expect that the first sub-two hour marathon will be run sometime in the next 15 to 20 years.

The world's fastest distance runners today run a half-marathon in less than 58.5 minutes. Perhaps the only significant difference between these runners and the sub-two hour marathon runner of the future will be found in superior running efficiency: runners of the future will use less oxygen when running at these speeds. To achieve this, athletes will need to be living and training at high altitude, or at least living in altitude chambers that replicate high-altitude conditions. Like today's top performers, they will combine an ability to handle heavy training loads with the intelligence of understanding the importance of recovery and of maximising performance by having the best possible diet and fluid intake before and during competition.

The sub-two hour runner will also train in a group of other world-class runners, as indeed Makau was doing; he will have a strong management support team able to provide the best medical and physiological back-up and arrange reliable pacemakers for the competition. He will be wearing optimal personalised racing shoes. Most importantly, he will have the self-belief that the record is within his reach.

Writing his autobiography more than 30 years ago, Britain's former world 10,000m-record holder Brendan Foster predicted that athletes of the future would continue to set new records not by running more miles but rather by training more smartly. By this, Foster was alluding to use of better scientific knowledge about distance running and to a greater emphasis on race-specific conditioning work. This still rings true today. Breaking the two-hour barrier for the marathon will require a phenomenal amount of hard work and discipline; it is also likely to draw more impetus from a better understanding and application of the science of peak performance.

Patrick Makau on his way to a world record
of 2:03:38 in Berlin in September 2011

IF THINGS
GO WRONG

THE PROBLEMS OF INJURY
AND OVER-TRAINING

Have you ever wondered whether getting injured is more a case of bad luck or bad planning? Sometimes – as discussed on pp. 194–196 – the cause of the injury is beyond your control. Three weeks before the 1992 Olympic Trials, for instance, I picked up a nasty knee injury when I was knocked over by a youngster charging across from the in-field on to the athletics track where I was doing a hard interval session. On other occasions, however, we run a greater risk of getting injured simply because we fail to act sensibly. We expect too much from our bodies and we fail or even refuse to heed the warning signs that our bodies are reaching the point of overstrain. (For an example of a runner succumbing to injury in this way, see Tony's story, pp. 139–141.)

Our chances of maintaining injury-free training would be much greater if we were all full-time athletes. Then – in theory, at least – we would have more time to rest and fewer things to worry about outside training. This does not get around the problem that most runners either don't enjoy this luxury, or, if they do, are on occasion prone to act in a manner which – in view of the stresses they are already imposing on their bodies – they will come to regret afterwards. Once, for instance, I gave myself a serious back injury at the end of a hard day's training in the process of changing a flat tyre on my car. Had I acted with less haste and a bit more common sense, I might have avoided the injury. The reality is that nearly every runner you meet will be able to give you at least one instance where for one reason or another they have succumbed to injury. Yet while injuries may be hard to avoid, some runners have learned better than others how to minimise the risk of breakdown. If you can learn the knack of steering clear of injury, you will enjoy more consistency in your training and competition, and with consistency you will find success.

The going gets tough in London

133

MONITORING YOUR CONDITION

There are a number of ways in which you can receive information about how well your body is coping with the stresses imposed on it. The most important means, but not always the most reliable, is your own sense of judgement: you should learn to 'listen' to your own body. If you feel an ache or pain that appears to be something more than just tired legs, it may be better to take a few days off rather than run with the problem and make it worse. It's better to be safe than sorry.

A useful way of measuring your state of overall tiredness is to take your resting pulse each morning soon after you have woken up. If it is more than 5–8 beats above normal, you should consider taking things very gently or even having a day off running.

By asking for advice from a coach (or a friend who understands your response to training), you can obtain a more objective assessment of your condition. This can be especially helpful if you are uncertain about either

VIEW FROM THE ROAD
Peter Knee: listening to your body

Peter Knee on the lessons learned in his debut marathon
Until 2010 half-marathons had been my limit and seemed tough enough. Then I decided to try the 'big one' and set myself a time goal of 3:45. As my training progressed, things seemed to be going so well that I decided to revise this goal to 3:20. But with just over a month to go to race day, I got busy at work and started to feel tired, even though my training load had reduced to not much more than one long run each week. With a week remaining to race day I came down with a cold, which developed into an ear infection and a back problem – I couldn't believe my luck! However, on race day I was back to feeling like my old self. I wanted to run at 7.30 min/mile but I knew that my own adrenalin and the speed of other runners at the start would increase this. I set off with the 7.15 min/mile pacemaker, so just inside 3:15 pace. At mile 14, as the temperature started to rise, I decided to slow down, but it was too late. At mile 16 I stopped and walked, knowing that I was overheated. At mile 18 I thought about giving up but then thought again. At mile 23 I saw my family for a second time, feeling even worse than when I first saw them around mile 16. One of my sons ran with me for a mile which was a huge help. I finally crossed the line in 3:36, way outside my 'dream' goal, but still very pleased to have finished.

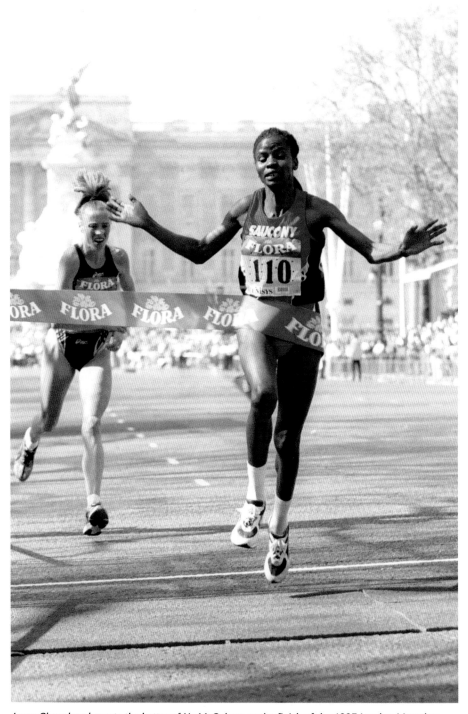

Joyce Chepchumba gets the better of Liz McColgan at the finish of the 1997 London Marathon (see p.118 for Liz's story of the race)

Q&A WHEN SHOULD I SEEK PHYSIOTHERAPY AS OPPOSED TO JUST TAKING REST?

It can be hard differentiating tiredness and tolerable pain from serious injury, and for the committed marathon runner there is always a fine balance between being too cautious and risking more serious problems by overriding some of the body's more obvious signals. One safety measure outlined in this chapter is to take an extra day of rest as a way of assuring yourself that tiredness is just that and not something more serious. If pain persists for more than a few days, especially after taking rest for 3–4 days, it may be wise to check out your problem with your GP – especially if you are fortunate to have a GP with a sports medicine background – or with a sports physiotherapist.

VIEW FROM THE ROAD
Bridget Davey: How I overcame injury

Bridget Davey learns the importance of rest and recovery

For me, the key to avoiding injury and over-training was learning about how to find the right balance between hard work and recovery.

Ever since I took up running, I have rarely had any problems motivating myself to go out for a run. Also, as my times have come down, my expectations about my results have increased. Enthusiasm and expectations are fine, but I've also had to learn to temper those with the knowledge that I'm not going to make massive improvements overnight.

In training for my first marathon some years ago I became so passionate about my running that I ignored some of the warning signs that I was doing too much. I started to get stiffness in my calf, first after some hard runs and then after most training runs, and didn't want to believe that it was getting worse. Eventually, two weeks before the marathon, I had to take the hard decision of withdrawing from the race. That experience, and regular massage, have since helped to reduce the number of injuries I've had. I've also learned to adopt a more flexible approach to training, following my urge to go out for a long run over the Downs while at the same time trying to listen to what my body is telling me in terms of rest and recovery afterwards.

the content or timing of your next training session. Athletes themselves are notoriously bad, for instance, at giving themselves a day off from their set schedule. While you might not notice your increasingly weary looks, hopefully your coach will.

In the case of serious injury, you should have your condition examined by a specialist. Here it can be particularly helpful if you have access to a trusted therapist who can diagnose your problem when it first arises, and then advise you on the best course of treatment.

SUPPORT SERVICES FOR THE ELITE

- *Medical screening.* I have found it useful to have regular check-ups with physiotherapists, physiologists and doctors – even when things appear to be going well. Having information relating to my normal level of fitness makes comparisons more meaningful when I might suspect that things are going wrong.
- *Blood testing.* Ever since I started training at altitude, I have had regular blood tests on my return home. I now have information on these values going back over the past 10 years, a useful bank of data for when problems arise.
- *Other support services.* Today, elite athletes are also able to enjoy support from a range of personnel including nutritionists, podiatrists and psychologists. The increasing importance given to these support services is a reminder – even to the amateur runner – that optimum performance depends on more than just the athlete's training workload.

Seeking out good advice remains a fine art, even for the most determined athlete. Throughout my career as an international athlete, I was helped by the fact that my coach had a good grasp of issues relating to illness and injury arising from his own competitive experience. I also enjoyed the support of two of Britain's best physiotherapists, Mary Bromiley and Neil Black. On numerous occasions I was able to avoid more serious problems because of their skill in diagnosing and treating my injury.

Mary's remedies for some of my injuries were as amazing as her diagnostic skills. When I had a chronic hamstring problem, for instance, I resorted to running some of my repetitions on the track in the reverse direction to reduce the strain on my weaker outside leg. On another occasion when I was trying to address the same weakness in my right leg, I was advised to wear ankle

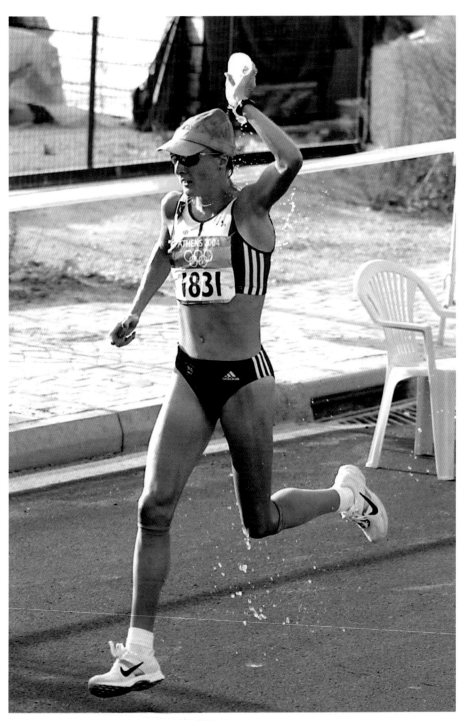

In the 2004 Athens Olympic Marathon Paula Radcliffe suffered from violent mid-race cramps, causing her to drop out 4 miles from the finish weights and swim side-stroke in the pool. Within a two-week period I began to see improvements in my condition. Time and again, Mary's advice proved invaluable in getting me back to pain-free running. Both Mary and Bruce have taught me that the best way to recover from an injury is not always to take complete rest. Often, it involves a programme of low-impact training such as cycling or pool running; or a series of strengthening exercises; or some hill walking progressing to light jogging on soft surfaces. These rehabilitation measures also have the advantage of maintaining a degree of fitness while at the same time overcoming the injury.

> **'Ultimately, you must take responsibility for the way you train and ensure that its toughness is tempered by large doses of common sense.'**

Coaches and athletes should not underestimate the importance of this kind of support. When things are going well, an athlete's 'support team' may appear superfluous to their immediate needs. However, when things start to go wrong, they often have a crucial role to play. At the same time, as the athlete you need to recognise that good advice is no guarantee against succumbing to injury. Ultimately, you must take responsibility for the way you train and ensure that its toughness is tempered by large doses of common sense. You must spare no effort in your determination to steer clear of injury and illness, the two hazards in running that have been the undoing of many promising athletes.

BAD LUCK OR BAD PLANNING?
Tony's story

Since the beginning of January, Tony had been training hard for London. It wasn't easy fitting an 80-mile-a-week training schedule around a demanding job that involved long hours in the office and occasional trips overseas. On weekday mornings he did a 45-minute run before getting to the office by 8.30a.m.; and his second run was done in the dark when most ordinary folk had their feet up in front of the TV. Tony was not the only one having to make sacrifices. His girlfriend hardly saw anything of him, and was now looking forward to the time after the marathon, when weekends would not be spent either training, racing or catching up on lost sleep.

With five weeks to go to the marathon, it looked as though the hard work was beginning to pay off. Despite being in the middle of a hard training period, Tony still found the energy to run two half-marathon races on consecutive weekends without significantly changing his normal training routine. In the first race he ran 1:12:20 and, in the second, 1:11:04. His goal of improving on his marathon best of 2:28 still seemed within his reach.

An exhausted Dan Robinson reaches the finish at the 2011 Brighton Marathon

With just one more week of hard training before the start of his taper, Tony was beginning to feel the strain. What made matters worse was that at the end of a busy week at work, he had to make a four-hour car journey to get to a family wedding on the following day. On the day after the wedding, he was due to run a relay leg for his club that involved another four-hour drive to get to the race, before returning home at the end of the weekend. Tony was also keen to do his last long run this weekend, and the only time available for this seemed to be on the Saturday morning before the wedding. He would then have to race with tired legs on the Sunday.

Not surprisingly, by Monday Tony was feeling a little worse for wear. On his run on Tuesday, he felt a sharp pain in his hip. By the end of the week, he was in so much pain that he could not even walk without a feeling of pain. It took another three weeks for Tony to get back into his running, by which time the marathon had passed – and with it, Tony's hopes of achieving what he had worked so hard for, for so much of the winter.

Tony's experience is one of those many 'bad luck' stories. But how much was it really a case of bad luck? To what extent could his injury be put down to misjudgement? Clearly it was not a great idea to couple a 20-mile long run with a hard race the following day. Should he not have modified his training plans on a weekend when he would be spending over 10 hours sitting at the wheel of his car? Could he not, for instance, have delayed his long run until the following Tuesday evening – even if this meant one fewer speed session with his usual training partners at the club?

KEY POINTS

- Plan your training sensibly and anticipate where tiredness might affect your ability to train well
- Learn ways of detecting when your body might be in need of a rest
- Take advantage of medical teams and other specialist services if they are available
- Practise the art of avoiding injury
- Spare no effort in your determination to overcome injury.

USEFUL TIPS
The art of avoiding injury

What steps can you take to reduce the risk of injury? How can you become better at detecting signs of over-tiredness? Here are some pointers to help you stay on the right side of injury.

- *Warm up properly.* Before a session of faster running, this should include some easy jogging (to raise your heart rate and body temperature) followed by some gentle stretching, during which you concentrate on the muscle groups that will be put under strain during your workout or race. This process should last a total of 20–30 minutes, at the end of which your body should be feeling warm and your muscles loose. Finally, run a few relaxed strides. By preparing in this way, you are cushioning your body from the shock of moving from rest to exertion, and thus helping it to operate more effectively. You also reduce the risk of getting injured.
- *Warm down adequately.* The above applies here too, only now you also aim to disperse some of the waste products (e.g. the lactic acid) that have accumulated during your exertion. This is achieved by doing 10–15 minutes of easy jogging at the end of your workout or competition. Your muscles contract as they cool down, so some gentle stretching after your warm-down jog will reduce the feeling of post-exercise stiffness.
- *Recognise the importance of rest* in your overall training programme (see also Chapter 4). You build fitness through a process of stress and recovery, stimulus and response. Don't try to take shortcuts.

- *Respect your own limitations*. Just because another runner is able to cope with a load of training doesn't necessarily mean that you will be able to, or that it will benefit you to follow the same programme.
- *More is not always better*. More training does not always equate with a higher level of fitness. Sometimes, what you may need first is more time to recover from your last hard workout before you can run your next hard session.
- *Don't play 'catch-up'*. If you do have to miss a few days' training because of an injury, resist the temptation to make up for lost workload by increasing your training load once you are back running.

The art of overcoming injury

The first and most important step towards overcoming an injury is to determine the nature and cause of the problem. Musculoskeletal causes of injury include:

- muscle weaknesses or loss of flexibility (e.g. calf or hamstring strains). These weaknesses increase the likelihood of postural instability and imbalances between different muscle groups, which in turn can result in problems in other parts of your body (e.g. in the hip and lower back)
- overloading, in the form of prolonged stress or small repetitive stresses (e.g. stress fractures in the lower limbs and feet)
- sudden wrenching or dislocation (such as ankle sprains).

The 'environmental' factors that can influence the chances of injury include:

- running surface or terrain (e.g. Achilles problems and shin splints, which are often associated with running on hard surfaces; sore quads from checking your speed when running downhill)
- inadequate or poorly-fitting shoes (e.g. causing blisters or sore knees)
- insufficient warm-up leading to muscle strains
- dietary habits (e.g. severe dehydration or glycogen depletion may cause muscle cramps).

Once you have diagnosed your injury – which might involve seeking the advice of a specialist – you are then in a better position to treat it. Some minor injuries can be treated with self-help remedies. Depending on the nature of the injury, these might involve:

- taking anti-inflammatory tablets or using a cream to subdue the feeling of pain, if soreness persists after training
- following the first-aid measures known by the acronym RICE (Rest–Ice–Compression–Elevation), to reduce swelling and bruising in the first 48 hours

- warming the affected area, then following this with some gentle stretching and massage (48 hours after contracting the injury)
- for blisters, draining the fluid, and keeping the area dry and clean – consider also using 'second-skin' plasters. The chance of blistering can be reduced by using vaseline and tape
- replacing your running shoes if the tread or cushioning is badly worn – usually after 800–1000 miles of running.

Many running-related injuries will heal within three to seven days, during which period you will not lose much fitness. It's important that you deal with your injury as soon as it arises, even if this means taking a few days off running: this will better serve your fitness in the long term. Remember also to graduate your return to normal training. Treatment of these and more chronic injuries should also be addressed by following specific muscle-strengthening and stretching routines.

When in doubt about the nature, cause or treatment of an injury, always consult your doctor or sports physiotherapist.

Rehabilitation from injury in 1995 involved daily ice baths for my feet

OVERCOMING INJURY
GOTHENBURG, AUGUST 1995

As I walked the short distance to the stadium, I glanced back towards the Information Tower that stood in the centre of the Athletes' Village. The temperature gauge read 32°C. Today, Saturday 14 August, was the hottest day yet of the week's competition at the 1995 World Championships in Gothenburg – and within a couple of hours, I would be lining up for the start of the marathon.

SURVIVING THE HEAT
I didn't lack the confidence to run well in hot conditions. At previous major championships – such as the European Championships in Split in 1990, in the World Championships in Tokyo in 1991 and in Barcelona in 1992 – I had experienced hot and humid weather and had survived as well as anyone else. I had the recent memory of running a marathon in warm Scandinavian sunshine from the previous year's European Championship Marathon in Helsinki.

The problem more likely to affect my performance on this warm afternoon was of a more fundamental nature. A chronic foot injury that I had first felt during a training trip to Kenya earlier in the year meant that my preparation for this race had been far from perfect. Though I was in good racing shape, my endurance training had been compromised: I had done only two long runs of over two hours in the three months leading up to the marathon.

The hot conditions ensured that the race got off to a slow start. A large group of over 20 runners reached the halfway point in 1:06:52. After 27km of running, the Brazilian Luiz dos Santos put in a surge which split up the leading pack. Initially I struggled to keep up with the breakaway group, though over the next three kilometres I slowly managed to close the gap and regain contact with the leaders. After another surge from the leaders I again fell off the pace, and soon found myself running in an isolated sixth place some 100m behind the leaders.

Up at the front, the European champion Martin Fiz was battling it out with the twice London Marathon champion Dionisio Ceron. Fiz eventually came out on top, but only after overturning a 20m deficit just three miles out from the finish. I ran the last 12km of the race on my own, gradually falling further behind the leaders. To rub salt into my wounds, a few miles before the finish I was passed by the third of the three Spaniards who had beaten me a year earlier in Helsinki: here they finished first, fifth and sixth. I finished seventh, the second British runner home, behind Peter Whitehead in fourth place.

This had been my toughest marathon yet. I knew I could do better – if only I could sort out the injury that had restricted much of my training in the preparation for the race.

SUCCUMBING TO INJURY

The first hint of a problem had come on my return from a winter training trip to Kenya, when I began to feel some discomfort underneath my right forefoot.

The pain grew worse as I trained harder in preparation for a marathon in March of that year. Immediately, I had sought out the advice of my physiotherapist Mary Bromiley. Fearing that I might have a stress fracture, Mary referred me to a specialist for a bone scan the following morning. When nothing showed up on the scan or subsequent MRI, she advised me to run only on soft surfaces until the discomfort disappeared.

A month later I had run my first marathon of the year in a big-city race in South Korea. After 26 miles of pounding on tarmac, my right foot was not surprisingly badly swollen – but I felt confident that a month's break from hard training following the marathon would give me a chance to sort out the problem for good.

However, when I resumed training in mid-April, the discomfort in my foot had not abated. This prompted

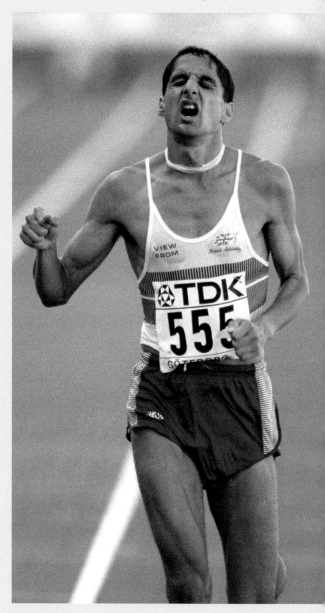

My toughest marathon yet, at the 1995 World Championships in Gothenburg

145

Mary to suggest a period of barefoot running on sand to reactivate the use of the tendons around the swollen area. But the numbing effect of running on frozen sand on a Devon beach in April proved to be more a relief than a cure and I was left searching for another remedy.

Over the next two months I put up with the pain as best I could and resigned myself to feeling discomfort every time my right foot hit the ground. Whenever I tried any really fast running – such as a session of fast 400m repetitions on grass – the pain became acute. Similarly, whenever I did a long run, my foot became so inflamed that I had to resort to twice-daily ice foot baths. Even driving my car began to irritate the problem. Meanwhile I continued my search for a cure by consulting with a range of specialists.

At the end of May I had a cortisone injection to reduce the inflammation in my swollen foot. I went back to train at altitude at Font Romeu where for the first 10 days I did all my training in the pool or on an exercise bike. The injection took away the pain and allowed me to complete three weeks of hard training for the remainder of my stay at altitude. I then returned home to test out my fitness.

During July I recorded some good race performances over distances from five to 10 miles, including a 10-mile win in 46:19. The discomfort underneath my right foot was still there, but I was able to control the pain with regular massage and ice baths.

On the day of the championship race in Gothenburg I felt optimistic about my chances of racing well. But optimism can be a poor substitute for the kind of confidence that is built on weeks of consistent, injury-free training.

OVERCOMING INJURY

The disappointment of my performance in Gothenburg made me even more determined to find a diagnosis for my injury. Though I had begun to fear that I might have to live with the frustration of running with this irritation, I also knew that without a cure I would have little chance of achieving my goals. To this end I continued to visit a number of specialists in the month following the marathon.

At the start of September 1995 I was discussing my problems with Dieter Baumann, with whom I had trained the previous winter in Kenya. Dieter had himself recovered from a serious foot injury in 1993, so was able to give me the name of the Dutch specialist, Peter Vergouwen, who had treated him. I immediately got on the phone to my friends in Holland, who offered to arrange an appointment for me. Within a week I was in his clinic in Utrecht. At last I felt I was starting to make progress towards resolving the problem.

Peter diagnosed the cause of the problem as a bone growth on the lateral side of my big toe, which was forcing the second toe to twist and rub against the third toe. He gave me two options. The first involved stopping running for six weeks to let the inflammation subside, during which time I would do a number of foot exercises as well as continuing with treatment before a further appraisal was made of the situation. The second involved surgery that would require a three-month rehabilitation period comprising six weeks of no running and a further six weeks of gradually reintroducing running training. Before surgery could be performed I would also have to wait two weeks for the inflammation to die down. Since the second option was more radical – and the first appeared to be similar to how I had been treating the problem thus far – I decided to opt for surgery.

When it came to finding a surgeon to carry out the operation, I wasn't short of help. Coming from a family of doctors, my brother-in-law recommended an orthopaedic surgeon with whom he was currently training in Bristol. After an initial consultation, a date was fixed for the operation and the offending bone was removed on 4 October 1995.

REHABILITATION
Then the process of rehabilitation got underway. This involved weeks of running and swimming in the pool, cycling and a programme of strengthening exercises. Over one 10-day period in December, my average daily training consisted of a 1200m swim, a 60-mile bike ride, 45 minutes of running in the pool, 30 minutes of gym work and some easy walking. I soon began to look forward to the day when I would be back into my normal running training.

I was glad to reach the end of 1995; it had been a frustrating year. For the last three months of the year, during an intensive period of rehabilitation, I had done hardly any running. For a much longer part of the year before this I had lived with the uncertainty of not knowing either the cause of or the cure for my injury. Despite all the help and encouragement I had received, I had started to doubt whether I would ever be able to perform at my best again. Finally, the injury had been diagnosed and eliminated. I could now move on and look ahead with confidence to my next race.

PART TWO

AIMING FOR THE TOP

*Mary Keitany crosses the line to record
her first victory in London in 2011*

PERIODISATION

A FULL YEAR'S PROGRAMME

If you are a regular runner, you might aim to complete one marathon each year. The London Marathon in April, or New York in the autumn, may become your main focus for part of your training year.

But once you have run your marathon and enjoyed a well-deserved rest period afterwards, there is still plenty of time in the remaining part of the year for you to enjoy your running and benefit from your fitness.

So how can you get the most out of this period of non-marathon training? Runners adopt different approaches to both training and competition once they have run their marathon. Some like to take advantage of their marathon fitness in the months following, by competing in races over shorter distances. Others prefer to take a break from structured training and are happy to run, either competitively or just for fitness, when time and inclination allow.

It is often the case that you won't know exactly what you will feel like doing until your marathon is behind you. Whatever you choose to do, you may find it helpful to have a plan for the remaining part of the year – even if the plan consists of not following a specific training programme.

ADVANTAGES OF PERIODISATION

There are several advantages to structuring, or 'periodising', your training:

- It helps you to focus on short-term goals
- It keeps you motivated
- It decreases the risk of over-training or burnout
- It gives you time to work on your weaknesses as well as your strengths
- It enables you to peak at the right time.

Andy Vernon (in the red vest of Aldershot and Farnham) has been one of Britain's top cross-country performers in recent years

Focusing on short-term goals

Periodising your training will allow you to focus on some short-term goals within given periods of the year.

It is sometimes hard to stay motivated to perform at your best if you go from one race to the next without any clear long-term plan. Breaking up your training year into phases with short-term goals is one way around this problem. Achieving these short-term goals may also act as a spur towards tackling your main long-term goal for the year.

During the two years I spent as a student in the States, the focus of my training was determined largely by the seasons of the US running calendar. The cross-country season got going at the end of the summer and lasted through the autumn. Once winter set in we ran indoor track until late February, which was then followed by outdoor track in the spring. Each phase of the year lasted approximately three months, an ideal time to stay motivated and focused on a specific goal at the end of each short season.

When I started to concentrate on marathon running, the other seasons in my training year became less of a priority. I still wanted to be running well in these periods, but I used them more as a means of developing my ability as a marathon runner rather than as an end in itself. This was also partly because the training involved in a marathon build-up was at times so demanding that I couldn't expect to be able to perform with an equal level of commitment at other times of the year.

'Don't tell them I'm feeling so good,' says eventual race winner Imane Merga of Ethiopia, midway through the 2011 World Cross-Country Championship 12km race

The other seasons of the year were when I did my background training for the marathon. For example, in a period of cross-country training leading up to the start of a marathon build-up, I would do more hill workouts. Alternatively, if this period came in the early summer I would concentrate on doing some good track workouts before moving back to the road. I enjoyed these phases of non-marathon training because they were times in the year when I put less pressure on myself to be at my peak of fitness.

Staying motivated
Periodising your training will help you stay motivated and keep excited about your training.

I'm a great believer in variety. At the time of my first marathon in 1993, I was still competing at a high level on the track and country. Following my first marathon in May 1993 I took part in a few track races over the rest of the summer. Then I got back into marathon training for the World Cup race in late October, after which I resumed cross-country training. I loved the variety because it stimulated me in different ways.

Even today when I go out running, I rarely run in the same place more than once a week. While running in familiar places has its own pleasures, varying the terrain and scenery of my runs helps to motivate me to get out the door as I go through the week. In the same way, it's also possible to vary the pattern of your training as you go through the year. You can run on different surfaces – road, track or country. You can run different kinds of workouts – tempo runs, speed sessions or hills. At certain times of the year, it may also be beneficial to replace or supplement some of your running training with some cycling or swimming as an alternative way of keeping fit.

Avoiding burnout
Periodising your training can help to recharge your batteries.

Remember that rest is as important as rigour. Just as you can benefit from having a number of days of easy running in the course of a tough month of marathon training, in the same way a low period of training at a given stage in the year can help refresh you in time for another period of focused effort.

Addressing weaknesses
Periodisation gives you the opportunity to concentrate on any specific areas of weakness.

Circuit training or a programme of light weights might not be every runner's idea of fun, yet it can form an important backdrop to your running. When used sensibly, it allows you to work on certain weaknesses that may cause you injury when you are back into a full programme of running training. Common areas of concern among distance runners are the muscles in the trunk and

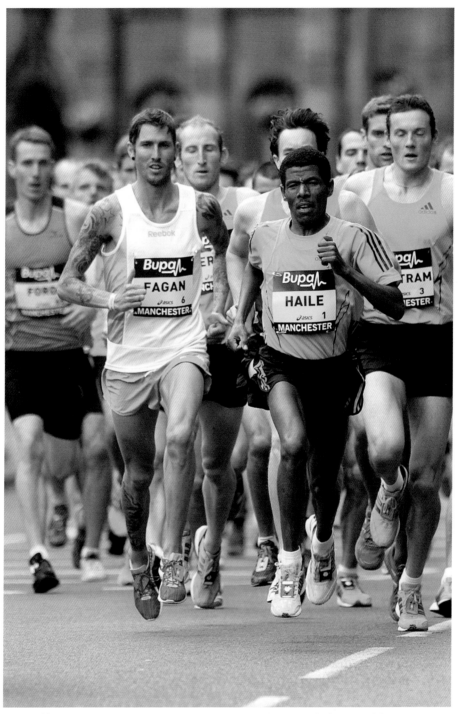

Outside his heavy marathon training periods Haile Gebrselassie regularly stepped down in distance to compete in shorter races - here at the 2011 Great Manchester Run 10km

lower back, and the hamstrings, gluteals and quadriceps. (For ideas on how to structure a suitable programme of weights or circuits, *see* pp. 214–215.)

Peaking at the right time

Periodising your training also helps you to retain a sense of purpose as you go through the year.

I have always been motivated by the desire to perform at my best on occasions when it matters most: the challenge has been to raise my game for the one big performance. I find it easier to do this if I've invested a lot of effort, both physically and mentally, during the process of preparation for competition. Structuring your training and racing in such a way that it leads towards such a climax is one way of sharpening your focus on that all-important goal. After all, for the marathon runner there is only one day that really counts.

HOW DOES PERIODISATION WORK?

The aim of a periodisation plan for your training year should be to bring you to the start of your marathon build-up in a reasonable state of fitness – while still feeling fresh and ready for the demands of training ahead of you. So, for instance, if you are planning to run a marathon in the spring, the main part of your build-up will take place in the months of January, February and March. Working back from the start of your build-up, December would be a good time to develop a base of fitness without putting too much pressure on yourself to follow a specific training programme.

The period preceding this at the end of the autumn would be a good time, if you needed it, to have a relatively quiet period of training. This might be the case if you had been racing frequently throughout the summer and early part of the autumn. To vary your training for the rest of the year, you may decide to concentrate on improving your times over shorter distances in the summer, either on the track or the road. Alternatively, you may choose to do some conditioning work by replacing your normal running training with some strength work in the gym (e.g. circuits or weights) – *see* also pp. 214–215.

Table 8.1 is an example of how to periodise your training year. It is geared towards reaching your peak in time to run a marathon in April.

Note, however, that there is no single plan to suit everyone. Work out what best fits around your preferences and your lifestyle. Obviously, if you're a regular runner and have found a pattern of training that has worked well in the past, it may be best to continue with the same routine. Equally, there may be times when your training will benefit from a change. Adopting a different pattern to your training might stimulate you in new ways and provide a fresh challenge.

TABLE 8.1 AN EXAMPLE OF HOW TO PERIODISE YOUR TRAINING YEAR

Timetable	Type of training	Major goal
May/June/July	Emphasis on faster running over shorter distances. Include some track work	5km and 10km races
First half of August	Low period of training	Enjoy a break from the routine of training
Aug/Sep	Increase mileage and use 10km to 10 mile races to build fitness	Half-marathon race
Nov/Dec	Maintain long run, but reduce mileage and include hill work and circuits	Cross-country races
Last 10 days of Dec	Low period of training over Christmas	Recharge your batteries
Jan/Feb/Mar	Marathon build-up – period of hardest training	April marathon
April/May	Taper for race, reduce training	Race well, then have a good rest

KEY POINTS

- Get the most out of your running by making a training plan for the whole year
- Create stimulus by concentrating on different aspects of training at different times of the year
- Reduce the risk of injury and over-training by giving yourself a rest period at some stage in the year
- Use your long-term plan to keep you focused on your major goals for the year
- Address weak parts of your body by doing some gym work, thus reducing the risk of injury.

VIEW FROM THE ROAD
Fiona Powell: breaking barriers

Fiona Powell runs a big PB in the 2011 Berlin marathon

I took up running in 2007, off the back of a challenge to run a half-marathon. Within a year I ran my first marathon in just under 3 hours and 30 minutes. I have never looked back since. Very soon I was addicted to the endorphin rush of chasing PBs. By April 2010, with many more miles under my belt and a greater respect for the distance, I broke the three-hour barrier in London. In 2011 my main target was a marathon PB in Berlin. Earlier in the year I spent a few months trying to improve my 5km and 10km times before starting my 16-week marathon build-up. To achieve a PB I realised that I needed to increase my mileage and introduce more tempo runs. As the race drew closer, I was concerned that the higher mileage I'd been doing might have reduced the quality of my tempo and long rep sessions, but these concerns were put to rest when, one week out from the marathon, I ran a big PB for 5km. On race day I knew that good pacing was vital to achieve my goal. Berlin is so crowded over the first few kilometres that it forces you to start slowly. Within 10 minutes or so I was into my target pace and went through halfway in 1.23.02 – bang on target. The second half was much tougher: I had to keep my focus during a few tough stretches and I really appreciated the support of the crowds as my body started to hurt in the race's final quarter. Pushing hard all the way to the finish, I crossed the line feeling relieved and very happy, in a 7-minute PB of 2.46.15.

Fiona Powell in action in her build-up to the 2011 Berlin Marathon

USEFUL TIPS
Training with the seasons

To the non-runner, running might seem like a monotonous form of exercise. Once you get involved yourself, you soon realise that this need not be the case. You can find variety both in your training workouts and in the distances and surfaces on which you compete. Below are some suggestions for ways in which you can change the emphasis of your training and competition as you go through the year. For details of specific training sessions, you might need more specific advice from a coach; alternatively, refer to a running magazine such as *Runner's World*.

- *Spring/summer*. Speedwork: aim to run some short races over 5km, on either the track or the road. Alternate between workouts of a timed session on a running track (e.g. 400m/600m repetitions) and a less structured session (e.g. a fartlek with bursts of quicker running) in woods or parkland. Consider reducing the overall volume of your running, substituting it with some other exercise such as cycling.
- *Summer/autumn*. 10 km/10-mile racing: aim to improve your best times over these distances. Twice weekly workouts on road or grassland and a longish run (of 10–12 miles). After the summer holidays, this might be a good time to enjoy the company of runners from your local running club and to build up together towards a race.
- *Autumn/winter*. Strength and conditioning: if you're keen to keep up your running, why not try some cross-country races? Include some hill repetitions into your weekly training programme. Alternatively, replace some of your running training with a gym session of circuits, step machine or Nordic ski.
- *Winter/spring*. Marathon preparation: emphasis on endurance (especially the weekly long run). After your marathon, have some time off serious training. One of my favourite ways of taking active rest, for instance, is to go on a walking holiday.

THE ROAD TO BUDAPEST
BUDAPEST, AUGUST 1998

In 1997, I learned the hard lesson about training: that more is not always better. As a result of overdoing my training for the 1997 World Championship Marathon in Athens, I was forced to withdraw from the race and was unable to resume normal training for at least two months afterwards. (For a more detailed account of this experience *see* Chapter 11.) If the answer then was not to train harder, it seemed right to focus on different aspects of my build-up at different times of the year with the aim of bringing myself to a peak at the

TABLE 8.2 A MORE STRUCTURED APPROACH – PERIODISING TO PEAK FOR BUDAPEST

Timetable	Phases of the training year
Mid-September to late-October	Six weeks of strength work (stabilisation and other exercises for lower back/stomach), hills and threshold runs
Late-October to early-December	Five weeks of repetition and interval work, with introduction of cross-country races, followed by one easy week
Early-December to late-January	Seven weeks at altitude: one week easy after arrival, then focus on threshold runs, long reps and short intervals
Late-January to late-March	Eight weeks with focus on cross-country races, continuing in training with long reps and short intervals
First two weeks of April	Two weeks mid-season break; walking holiday
Mid-April to late-May	Start back with six-week programme circuits, building up mileage and introducing long reps on road
June	Start of 12-week specific build-up to marathon; three weeks at altitude: high volume and low intensity, followed by one week easy
July to early-August	Race at start of period, recovery, then into hardest training block of high-quality marathon-specific work
Early-August to 22 August	Start taper for marathon

right time. With this in mind I took a more structured approach to periodising my 1997–98 season – *see* Table 8.2. My goal was to be at my peak for the European Championship Marathon in Budapest in August 1998.

THE STRUCTURE OF THE YEAR

After attempting two marathons in 1997, I decided to run a full cross-country season in the winter of 1997–98. I planned to concentrate on general conditioning work in the autumn, and then to have a good period of hard running training over Christmas and the New Year. My main racing period would take place at the start of February, having set myself a mid-term goal of winning a place on the British team to take part in the World Cross-Country Championships in Morocco at the end of March.

As it turned out, though my training during the winter months appeared to go well, I had some disappointing races in February and March. I only managed to finish ninth in the British Cross-Country Trials and thus failed to win a place on the team for the World Championships. I decided, however, to stick to my overall plan and used the remaining part of March to do a series of road races over 5km and 10km, before taking a short break in April.

When I resumed training in the third week of April, there were still over four months to go to the marathon in Budapest. I started to build up my mileage, combining this with some more conditioning work – this would prevent me from doing too much running training in the early phase of the build-up. I planned to run two half-marathons in preparation for the European Championship Marathon. The first, at the end of May, would allow me to test my fitness before I went away to train at altitude. The second, in early July, would be midway through my build-up, and just before the hardest period of training planned for the final seven weeks before the marathon.

Both these races, and the training in the intervening period, went according to plan. I ran 1:03:45 and placed third in the first half-marathon. This was followed by three weeks of good training back at Font Romeu, during which I ran over 290 miles in the final 14-day period. Ten days after leaving altitude, I then ran the second half-marathon, and won the race in a time of 1:03:25. The final phase of my build-up took place at a training camp at Wellington College in July and the early part of August. Here I ran a number of marathon-specific sessions, including long runs of 35–45km and sustained tempo runs over 20–25km.

My race in Budapest was the culmination of 10 months of planning, training and competition. Despite one or two disappointments in the course of the year, I had not allowed these to distract me from the year's main focus of being in peak condition for my marathon at the end of August. The period of hardest training had taken place over the summer, in the three months prior to the race. With the help of a sports psychologist I had given careful consideration to my race strategy, and as the race approached I grew in confidence about my readiness to perform.

RACE DAY IN BUDAPEST

After a steady opening few kilometres, a Russian runner went into the lead and opened up a gap of over 50 seconds by the 15km point. Realising that the leader was increasing his lead, the chasing group of over 20 runners gradually started to increase the tempo. We passed halfway in around 1:07 and at 23km caught the Russian. We maintained a good pace for the next few miles, which brought us around to the start of the final 10km lap of the city centre before we headed back to the stadium. Running in the leading group, I was still feeling good but found it hard to assess how much I still had in reserve for the final part of the race. Nevertheless, I decided it was worth attempting to get ahead before we got too close to the finish. At 28km I made a surge to the front of the field, which quickly reduced the leading group to a pack of seven runners. Having run the 29th kilometre in 2:58, three Italian runners came past me and took over the lead. The next kilometre, which we covered in 3:00, was the point where I started to struggle to stay up with the leaders. The best I could do now, as I watched the leaders disappear further down the road, was to maintain my position. Running the last five miles in isolation, I entered the stadium in seventh place, was overtaken in the final 300m, and finished an exhausted and disappointed eighth in 2:14:02.

Reflecting on my level of fitness and the toughness of the opposition, I realised afterwards that my race strategy had been over-ambitious. I consoled myself with the thought that at least I had given my all – in training and competition beforehand, and in the race itself – achieved on the basis of a strategic year-round plan.

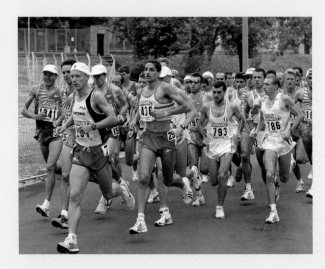

Setting off on my last championship marathon at the 1998 European Championships in Budapest

TACTICS AND STRATEGIES

Today's perceived wisdom about how best to run a marathon is to save your biggest effort for the end of the race. Run conservatively for the first half; treat the 20-mile point as 'halfway' in terms of effort; and race over the last six miles.

If you follow this approach, you will have a better chance of maintaining an even pace for the entire 26-mile distance. You might even achieve what few marathon runners are able to do – namely, to run the second half of the marathon faster than the first half, which is today described as running the marathon 'with negative splits'.

'GUN-TO-TAPE' OR 'BACK-TO-FRONT'?

Compare this with the tactics adopted by some of the great marathon runners of 40 or even 60 years ago. It was not unusual then for runners to try to win marathons by outrunning their opposition from the start of the race. Jim Peters in the 1950s, and Ron Hill in the 1960s and 1970s, won a number of their big marathons in this way. Frank Shorter employed a similarly aggressive approach in winning the 1972 Olympic Marathon. His race strategy involved putting in a surge early in the race and then managing to stay in front for the rest of the race.

Shorter's tactics were designed to give him a psychological as well as a physical advantage over his opponents: overcoming the opposition in order to win the race was the only thing that mattered. It was a tough way of running a marathon because it sometimes meant starting off at a pace that could not be maintained all the way to the finish. It was also unlikely to produce the quickest winning time.

The advent of mass-participation marathon races – starting with the first mass-participation New York Marathon in 1979 and followed by the first

Pacemakers are now a regular feature of big-city marathons

London Marathon in 1981 – signalled a change in how marathons were run and won by the elite. There were still instances of winning from the front – such as when Hugh Jones led every step of the way to win the 1982 London Marathon and when Steve Jones set a world record of 2:07:13 in the 1985 Chicago Marathon, covering the first half of the distance in 1:01:43 – but in general as the depth of competition increased and race organisers started to offer incentives for running fast times, the more aggressive style of frontrunning was replaced by the more conservative tactic of running most of the race at a level pace and then trying to speed up towards the finish. Such were the race strategies of some of the great marathon runners of the 1990s including Gelindo Bordin of Italy (1988 Olympic Marathon champion), Dionisio Ceron of Mexico (three-time winner of the London Marathon from 1994 to 1996) and the Spaniards Martin Fiz and Abel Anton, who both won world championship marathon titles in the 1990s. This trend has continued in recent years. Paul Tergat set his world record of 2:04:55 in the 2003 Berlin Marathon by running the second half of the race (61:54) more than a minute faster than the first half (63:01) while Haile Gebrselassie also achieved a 'negative split' of 61:57 following a first half of 62:29 when improving on Tergat's record in Berlin four years later.

RACE STRATEGIES FOR TODAY'S ELITE

Over recent years there has been an explosion of Kenyan distance runners onto the world marathon scene – in particular in the men's event – so that at big-city marathons it is not unusual to find Kenyans occupying more than half of the race's top ten positions. The depth of competition, particularly among these African runners, has also accentuated the trend towards fast finishes – even when Paul Tergat set a new marathon world record of 2:04:55 at the 2003 Berlin Marathon he was pushed all the way to the line by fellow Kenyan Sammy Korir, who finished just one second behind him. And it's not only the Kenyans who specialise in winning sprint finishes. Over a four-year period from 1999 to 2003 the Ethiopian athlete Gezahagne Abera won five of his

Q&A IS THERE ANY VALUE IN FRONTRUNNING?

The conventional wisdom of pacing may be true, but sometimes runners actually feel more comfortable leading a group of runners. Many of the world's great distance runners of the past, including Dave Bedford in the 1970s and Steve Jones in the 1980s, came from the school of frontrunning – and had considerable success at it.

six marathon titles (including the 2003 London Marathon) by a total margin of just seven seconds! Quick finishes are, however, less the norm on difficult marathon courses where the undulations of the course route (such as the famed 'Heartbreak Hill' in Boston or the final three miles through Central Park in New York) present more opportunities for runners to make their winning moves before the finish line is in sight.

In the women's event, the dominance of African marathon runners is less apparent and race strategies follow a less uniform pattern. While Britain's world record holder Paula Radcliffe fashioned her own style of frontrunning – in a number of her early marathons she led from gun to tape – there are plenty of other examples of races being decided over the second half of the distance, and particularly in the race's final quarter, as has been the case in many recent editions of big-city marathon races in London, Boston, Chicago and New York.

Pacemaking
Another feature of big-city marathons today, in contrast to the marathons of 20 or 30 years ago, is the role played by the pacemakers in the early stages of a race. The practice of using pacemakers as a means of achieving faster finishing times in middle- and long-distance races goes back many years. When Roger Bannister ran the first sub-four-minute mile in 1954, for instance, he was helped by two pacemakers, Chris Brasher and Chris Chataway, for three-quarters of the distance. But only in recent times have they become a regular presence in big international marathon races.

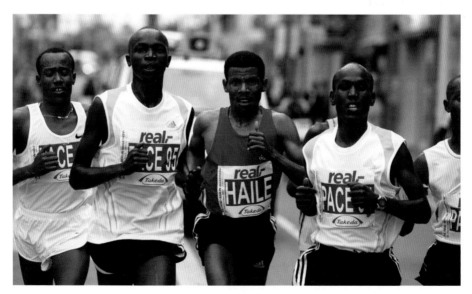

Haile Gebrselassie used pacemakers to good effect en route to his world record time of 2:04:26 in the 2007 Berlin Marathon

There are two main advantages of having another runner set the pace for you – one physical, the other psychological. The physical one is that due to reduced air resistance, it is easier to maintain a certain pace by running just behind, rather than in front of, another runner. Psychologically, the runner following also benefits from having one fewer thing to worry about: while the runner in front – or the 'front-runner' – keeps an eye on the stopwatch and modifies the pace accordingly, the runner behind can concentrate simply on running as efficiently as possible.

To what extent does pacemaking contravene the notion of athletics as an individual sport? While purists might complain, the only restriction placed on the practice of pacemaking by those who set the rules is that the pacemaking runner must be officially entered in the same race as the other runners who benefit, and that the pacemakers start the race from the race's start alongside those runners they intend to help.

Pacemakers are not, however, officially sanctioned in international championship competition: the contest is purely about winning medals and achieving high finishing places. (The hot conditions in which most major championship marathons are staged further weakens any incentive for the runners to chase fast times.) As a consequence, nearly all championship races are run at a slower pace than their big-city counterparts, with the runners concentrating more on their tactics than on sustaining their optimum pace.

PACEMAKERS: HELP OR HINDRANCE?

Even pacemakers can spring a surprise on the runners they are intended to help. In the 1994 Los Angeles Marathon, the official pacemaker Paul Pilkington took advantage of the other runners' reluctance to follow his pace by maintaining his lead all the way to the finish. Only after crossing the finish line two minutes behind Pilkington did the second-placed Italian athlete discover that he had not won the race – since Pilkington had not dropped out after his official duties were over.

In the 1999 London Marathon the leading contenders similarly decided not to follow the pacemakers. The gamble of the relatively unknown Moroccan Abdelkader El Mouaziz to pursue the rabbits paid off when after 17 miles (where the last of the three rabbits dropped out), El Mouaziz found himself with a lead of almost two minutes over the race favourites. Though the Moroccan slowed down in the final stages of the race, he still managed to reach the finish almost a minute ahead of his fast-finishing opponents.

In this respect, these races more closely mirror the marathon contests of 30 years ago, where the challenge lies as much in outwitting as in outrunning the opposition. (It is interesting that a few big-city marathon races, such as the elite women's race at the New York Marathon, do not use pacemakers as a deliberate attempt to highlight the competition over the need for fast times.)

That pacemaking has become such a regular feature of distance running at international level does pose problems for the sport. Most athletics enthusiasts watch the sport because of the fascination with man-to-man combat – 'Who is the world's fastest man?' rather than 'How fast can he run?' Not surprisingly, therefore, those races which do not depend on the participation of pacemakers, such as the major international championships, continue to attract the greatest excitement among the sporting public.

Commercial considerations

Aside from the advent of mass-participation competitions, the main difference between the marathon races of the 60s and 70s and those of today is the commercial aspect of competitions. At an international marathon staged in Holland in the mid-1950s, Jim Peters, who was then the world record holder for the distance, took home as his winning prize a portion of fine Dutch cheese bought for him by his accompanying team manager on their journey home – a far cry from the huge financial rewards on offer at today's big-city marathons.

Winners' prize money at today's big-city marathons is often in the region of $50,000–$100,000; appearance money may be easily twice that amount; and time bonuses for world record performances also reach into six-figure sums.

Race organisers are ready to offer large appearance fees to top athletes because the event's status depends largely on the number and quality of the elite athletes taking part. A stronger field of runners is more likely to produce fast winning times. Fast times – or even better a world-best performance – are in turn likely to generate more media interest and enhance the race's chances of attracting better sponsorship in future years. Higher revenue from sponsorship enables race organisers to entice runners to the following year's race – and a cycle of success is set in motion.

The rewards for elite athletes of a fast finishing time come in the form of bonus payments both from race organisers and their individual sportswear sponsorship contracts. A runner's finishing time may also determine the level of appearance money on offer at their next marathon. Consequently, many elite marathon runners have one eye on achieving the best possible finishing time while at the same time trying to win the race.

The desirability of producing fast times, both on the part of race organisers and runners, influences the pattern of many of today's big-city marathons. For at least the first half of the race the leading contenders run behind a group

PAULA RADCLIFFE'S TWO WORLD RECORDS

Competing in her third race over 26 miles, Paula Radcliffe won the 2003 London Marathon in a time of 2:15:25, the fastest time ever run by a female athlete for the marathon. For eight years this mark was considered as the official women's marathon world record. Then in 2011 the IAAF changed the rules, deciding that performances run only in women's-only races would be considered for world record purposes. Paula's time, run with the assistance of two Kenyan male pacemakers, became a world best mark for a 'mixed' race, while her time of 2:17:42 from the 2005 London Marathon was elevated to the official world record. This ruling, designed to push race organisers towards staging women's-only marathon races for elite female runners, appears to be a harsh decision on Paula's exceptional 2003 performance. With or without pacemakers – and, let's face it, all the recent men's marathon world records and record attempts have been made with the assistance of pacemakers for most of the distance – the marathon is essentially a race between the athlete and the distance. Support from pacemakers can help, by reducing air resistance and by taking away the concern of controlling the pace, but ultimately races are won and records broken as a result of individual effort and performance. To those who argue that the use of pacemakers prevents a fair comparison with earlier records set without pacemakers, I would answer that there are now plenty of other ways (such as improved shoe technology and nutritional aids) in which comparability does not fairly apply and which increase the likelihood of higher standards today.

of other runners, designated as the race's 'rabbits'. At a certain point in the race, the rabbits retire from the competition having done their pre-assigned task. It is only then that the race to the finish truly begins.

Though the involvement of pacemakers imposes a more predictable pattern upon the first half of a marathon, the race's outcome may remain far from certain – even up until the final mile. Sometimes a runner may try to surprise the opposition by getting clear of the field even before the rabbits have finished their job. On other occasions, the pace set by the race leaders drops temporarily at the point where the rabbits drop out, as the leading contenders take stock of their opposition and gather their strength for the race's final phase. Regardless of what happens in the first 20 miles, the last six miles of the marathon often produce dramatic swings in fortune for the leading runners as the race to the finish unfolds.

It's that close! After 42km, Kenyan Paul Tergat just gets ahead of Hendrik Ramaala in the 2005 New York Marathon (top) and Patrick Ivuti beats Jaouad Gharib in the 2007 Chicago Marathon (bottom)

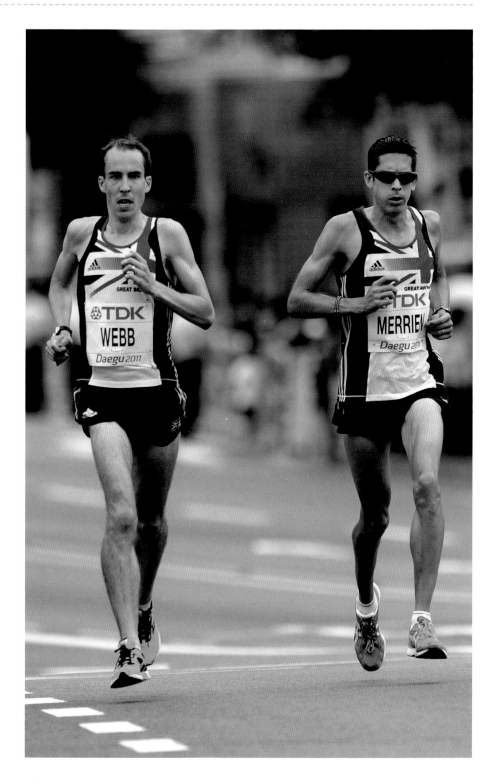

Thinking on your feet

No matter how hard and long you ponder all the possible scenarios, you will never be able to anticipate every likely turn in a race. So, as well as having a clear racing strategy before you start out, it's also important to be able to work out how best to run your race once the competition is underway. The way you decide to run your race is partly determined by the moves of your opponents, so you must be prepared to think clearly and react while on the run.

> **'Racing marathons has been described as a game of "chess on your feet", where one wrong move can prove costly.'**

My first marathon was a big-city one, and my main goal was to run a good time (sub-2:12), rather than to win the race. For the first 16 miles I ran my own race according to a set pace schedule, which meant falling behind the leading group of runners from the race's opening mile. After 16 miles my coach told me that I was rapidly gaining on the leaders, who had slowed down from their earlier brisk pace. Then I had to think about conserving my effort as I caught up with them, switching my focus towards trying to win the race. I eventually caught the leaders after 18 miles, ran with them for five miles, and put in a race-winning surge over the last three miles of the course.

My race strategy for the 1994 European Championship Marathon in Helsinki was based on my earlier two marathon victories. I planned to stay with the leaders until the final two or three miles, at which point I would make my run for home. My Spanish opponents, mindful of how I had won my two previous marathons, were keen to thwart any such ideas I had for this race and made a decisive move to get ahead of me at the 20-mile point. I failed to react to this move and any hopes I had of winning the race, or even a medal, quickly disappeared.

Racing marathons has been described as a game of 'chess on your feet', where one wrong move can prove costly. The art of being able to think and react under the pressure of competition is essential if you have ambitions to win the race. In marathon running, unlike chess, you suffer the consequences of your mistakes both in terms of fatigue and disappointment.

British marathoners Dave Webb and Lee Merrien in action at the 2011 World Championship Marathon in Daegu. Webb finished 15th and Merrien 22nd.

KEY POINTS

- Run at a level pace, or even with the intention of speeding up over the second half of the course, when aiming for the fastest possible time
- Learn the art of running strongly over the final section of the marathon
- Work out a clear racing strategy
- Anticipate how you would react to the moves of your opponents
- Learn the art of thinking on your feet under the pressure of competition.

VIEW FROM THE ROAD
Paul Halford: running a negative split

Paul Halford runs a negative split en route to a PB in London
I'm not sure what it is about the halfway point in the London Marathon, but it usually tends to 'wake me up'. In 2011, I reached the halfway point dead on schedule for my finishing goal of 2:30 but then, either because my Garmin went haywire among the tall buildings or because I missed a few mile markers (or was it simply that I got carried away?), I suddenly found I had speeded up by 5–10 seconds per mile. The consequence was that the last two miles became a real struggle. I didn't quite 'hit the wall', but I remember that every breath I took required a grunt. The result: a four-minute PB and a finishing time of 2:28:32. Having run big negative splits for two consecutive years, a lot of people told me that I had found the perfect way to run a marathon. I'm not so sure: running too cautiously can be just as bad as running too aggressively. But if you're going to get it wrong, I certainly know which way I'd find more pleasurable.

Ukrainian Sergei Lebid has been the most consistent European cross-country runner of the past decade

VIEW FROM THE ROAD
Aly Dixon: Achieveing your goals

Aly Dixon on achieving her time goal at the 2011 Brighton Marathon
My big goal for the 2011 Brighton Marathon was to run a time under 2:35:00, a big step-up from my existing PB of 2:42:50. I stayed in Kenya for two out of the three months of my main marathon build-up, doing a lot of hill running and sustained runs at marathon pace. I knew I was in great shape going into the marathon after recording PBs at shorter distances including a half-marathon of 72:30 and a 10km in 33:26. To help me prepare mentally for the race, I broke the course down into eight 5km segments coinciding with the eight drink stations. The time passes more quickly for me if I count the feed stations rather than the miles or kilometres. Also, I put flat coke in my drink bottle at 35km and know that once I've taken this drink I'm almost home. As part of my preparation I also make sure I know my target times for 10km, halfway and 20 miles. The tough part of the course in Brighton is in the first 10 miles, so I planned to start steadily, maintain a level pace to 20 miles, and then pick up the pace over the last 10km. I went through halfway at 76:50 feeling very strong, knowing that I was well inside my target finishing goal. I maintained this pace to 22 miles where, as I turned back to the finish along the sea front I hit the wind and my pace dropped. I had to work really hard over the next four miles but was able to finish strongly to record 2:34:50. It had been one of those races where everything came together on the day, including the weather.

Aly Dixon finishes strongly to win in Brighton with a new PB of 2:34:50

A FAST FINISH IN KOREA
KYONGJU, MARCH 1995

It was March 1995, and we had come to the southeastern corner of Korea for the Dong-A International Marathon. (Dong-A was the name of the Korean newspaper group sponsoring the race.) Formerly held in the capital, Seoul, with all the attendant problems of busy streets, traffic and pollution, the race had been moved a few years previously to Korea's ancient capital, Kyongju.

FAST TIMES
My last two marathons in Helsinki and San Sebastian had been championship races. Now I was looking for a race where I could run a fast time. My best time to date was 2:10:03 from the 1993 World Cup Marathon. Now, on a good course and with the right conditions, I felt I could run considerably faster than this.

Korea in March typically enjoys a climate that is ideal for marathon running: cool, dry and still. For the first five days of our stay in Kyongju we experienced precisely this kind of weather. Not only was it good marathon-running weather; it also made for pleasant afternoon sightseeing visits to the many Buddhist temples around the town, as we found our bearings amidst our new surroundings.

The Kyongju race lacked the mass appeal of its London or New York counterparts. In addition to the 60 runners taking part in the elite race, the event attracted only a further four or five hundred other runners. The main interest for the race organisers and sponsors was to produce a high-quality race at the front, with finishing times that ranked favourably against other big-city races. Indeed, the 1994 edition of the race had served this very purpose: Manuel Matias of Portugal (whom I had gone on to beat in the 1994 European Championship Marathon) had outsprinted the Korean home favourite Wan-ki Kim to win in a time of 2:08:33, the fourth-fastest winning time in the world in all marathons run that year.

COURSE CHANGES
Two days before the race, the international athletes were given a tour of the course. To our dismay we learned that a number of changes had been made to the previous year's course. In 1994 the race had started and finished in the town's athletic stadium. Now, to avoid the problem of congestion at the start of the race, the organisers had moved the start and the finish out on to the street in front of our hotel. But in doing this, they had also changed the route of the two-lap course, which now included three uphill sections.

The first stretch, a long drag of around 400m, came at the 8km point and was repeated at around 40km. The second, coming after 12km, was much more severe, in the form of a hill that rose for over a mile before descending just as steeply for the same distance on the other side. Not ideal for producing fast times! Worse news was in store as race day approached. Wintry weather was returning to the region, with blustery winds and a fall in temperature forecast for race day.

At the pre-race meeting of athletes, coaches and managers, the talk was still of aiming to reach halfway in around 1:04:00 for a finishing time inside the existing course record. The pace for the first half of the race would be set by the Polish runner Wieslaw Perszke.

I knew Perszke well from training-camp days at Font Romeu. He took a strictly commercial attitude towards his sport: to do well in running meant earning as much money as possible. Here, his pay cheque would come on the condition that as the designated rabbit he ran to time for the first half of the race.

RACE DAY IN KOREA

As forecast, Sunday 19 March 1995 turned out to be a cold (five degrees Celsius) and windy morning. The race got underway at 9.00a.m., with about 15 leading international runners settling in behind the pacemaker. Negotiating the first uphill section without any problems, we passed the 10km point in 30:23 – on schedule to run around 2:08:00 – and then we headed out towards the second, larger loop beyond the town limits.

As we approached the second hilly section of the course at 12km, our pacemaker Perszke suddenly stepped off the road unable to keep to pace. As a result we were left to make the pace ourselves. The tempo inevitably slowed as we ascended the long climb ahead of us. Although we accelerated down the other side, we were well behind schedule at the halfway point (reached in just outside 1:05).

At this point we turned into the most exposed part of the course and the pace slowed even more, with none of the runners in the leading group willing to take it up. We covered the 10km from 20km to 30km in 32:24 (slower than 2:16 pace). As we approached the last six miles of the race the leading group still comprised about 12 runners.

RACE TO THE FINISH

Knowing that big-city marathons often boil down to running fast for the first 20 miles and racing hard for the last six, my pre-race strategy had included an option of making a winning break at around the 32–34km mark. In the week leading up to the event, I had done some fast running on this stretch of the course as a form of race rehearsal.

The slower-than-expected pace for the first 20 miles of the race necessitated a change in race strategy. A run for home from six miles out with a dozen good runners on my shoulder would be a risky business. I decided to wait until around 35–37km before trying to strike out for the finish.

At 34km the local favourite Lee Bong-Ju (who went on to win the silver medal in the 1996 Atlanta Olympic Marathon) made a sudden surge to run ahead of the chasing group. Together with the Mexican runner Andres Espinosa, I immediately set off to catch him. One kilometre up the road we were back on the Korean's heels, at which moment Bong-Ju again accelerated and opened up a small gap. Espinosa and I tried desperately to hang on. On the approach to the last hill at 40km, the Korean finally saw us off with another race-winning surge. I was left to battle it out for second place, which I snatched from the Mexican in the final 200m of the race.

The quickest section of the race had been the last five miles, with the Korean running a 5km split to 40km of 15:05. The Korean's winning time was 2:10:58, I ran 2:11:03, and Espinosa 2:11:08. As the pace increased in the latter stages of the race, I had hung on well and was pleased to take second place. But it was disappointing that the race had not given us the opportunity to run at our fastest. The weather, the course and the pacemaking had failed to live up to our expectations.

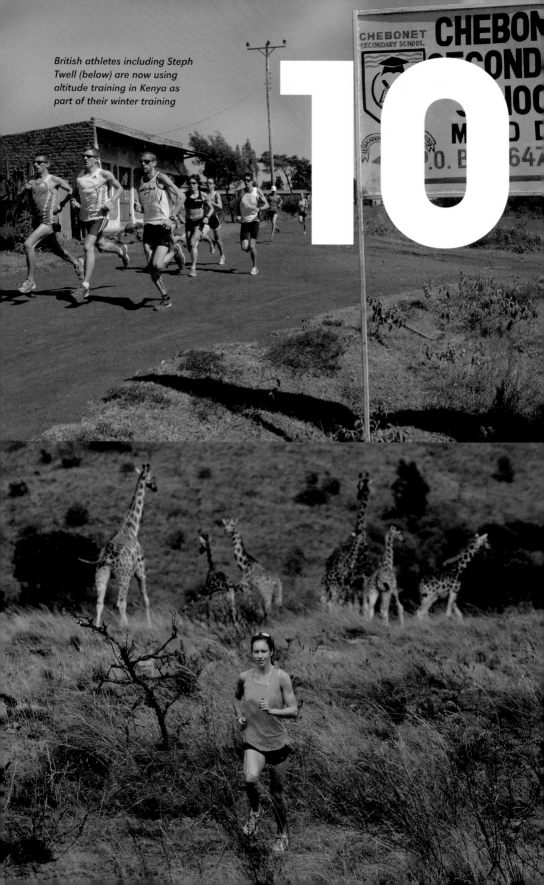

British athletes including Steph Twell (below) are now using altitude training in Kenya as part of their winter training

10

THE FULL-TIME ATHLETE

For most people, running is and will always remain a leisure activity. Though it demands great effort and fills you with ambition, it still remains a hobby – something you pursue to varying degrees of commitment purely for the love of it.

At the elite level, running is no longer a sport practised by amateurs. Gone are the days of Dave Bedford and Brendan Foster, heroes from my childhood days, when an athlete's training was fitted in around a normal day's work. Today's elite athletes are full-time professionals in their sport. Their whole lifestyle is geared around their training and competitive needs.

RUNNING AS A WAY OF LIFE

The process of devoting oneself single-mindedly to training and competition is enhanced when runners come together to live in a training-camp environment. The camp provides both for their training needs – the support of training partners and coaches – and for their needs outside training, such as meals, accommodation and medical support. In such an environment, away from the distractions of home and family life, athletes are able to focus on the task at hand: the continual daily cycle of training and recovery.

During my career as a full-time athlete I regularly experienced the rhythm of training-camp life. At the Italian National Olympic Training Centre in Tirrenia, near Pisa, for instance, I often got the feeling that a day involving nothing other than training, eating and relaxing was a perfectly normal way to live. This is how our day was structured:

- an early-morning breakfast would be followed by a strong coffee over the morning's sports newspapers
- training got underway at around 10.30a.m. and lasted until lunchtime
- after a good helping of Italian pasta and salad, we were ready for our afternoon siesta

- in the late afternoon we went into town for a quick espresso before returning for a second, lighter load of training
- gym work, Jacuzzi and massage were fitted in before another good meal in the evening.

A PRIVILEGE OF THE ELITE?

The good news for the amateur runner is that the benefits of training-camp life can be enjoyed by everyone – whatever your level of running. Though you might not have the time or money to indulge in your training to quite the same

VIEW FROM THE ROAD
Tim Cook: Running holidays

Tim Cook, a veteran of nine marathons and approaching 100 half-marathons, has been enjoying running holidays for the past 25 years
For myself and my wife Carol a running holiday combines our two great passions of running and travelling. Over the past 25 years these trips have taken us to 27 different countries (including Morocco, Malta, Ethiopia and Dubai), many of which I might never otherwise have thought of visiting. Family often asks 'Can't you take a holiday without a run?' Very occasionally we do, but more often the race gives a focus to the holiday and helps us set our travel dates. On short breaks the race itself may be the only run we do, with the rest of the time on the beach, or exploring, or boozing. In recent years our love of foreign runs has rubbed off on folks at our running club in Peterborough and over the last five years we have organised an annual group trip to places such as Palermo in Italy, Riga in Latvia and Ypres in Belgium. The club trips are a great way for members who don't usually run together to get to know each other as well as to introduce non-running partners. The trips have often created club stories which have become club folklore: the broken toilet in Malta, the member who has never shared with the same person twice and the number of couples who have come back pregnant.

The trips need not be expensive. Sometimes we do our own thing and at other times we use specialist running companies. When organising foreign trips and entering races overseas we have been able to mix the distances so that every race does not need to be a marathon or half-marathon. Our trips are accessible to all our members and the conversation on the way home usually comes back to 'Where are we going to next, Tim?'

EXPERT COMMENT
Mike Gratton: The benefits of a running holiday

Mike Gratton won the London Marathon in 1983 and now organises running tours for runners of all standards through his company, 2:09 events

Very few ordinary runners get the opportunity to train like a full-time elite athlete, but training camps, if only for a short period, give you the opportunity to experience being a full-time athlete. The intensity of full-time training at a running camp can give you a fitness boost about two weeks later, once the legs have been rested and the training absorbed after the holiday. It's also a chance to see how much you can achieve when you're able to rest between sessions and to enjoy the social banter of other athletes, rather than having to fit in sessions around an eight-hour working day and family commitments. Put simply, training camps are a chance to be indulgent about your running without having any guilty feelings.

extent as the full-time professional, this need not mean that you totally miss out on the experience. You can organise to spend a weekend away with other runners and get in on the act. It might even give you that extra spring in your stride for when you return to your normal routine.

BENEFITS OF TRAINING-CAMP LIFE

Some of the benefits that I have experienced from spending time in training-camp environments include:

- the company of training partners
- training in warm weather and at altitude
- more time to rest and recover
- access to coaching and medical support
- the opportunity to learn from others
- increased confidence and purpose about training.

GETTING INVOLVED

I first started going to training camps at the age of 12. Each year our school cross-country club held a pre-season training camp on a farm field just outside the village of Westwell in Kent. The camp lasted a week, comprising four days of twice-daily training and a day out in Margate, followed by an end-of-week relay on the Saturday before we travelled back home. Often, there were as many as 50 boys attending. We were divided up into teams to carry out campsite duties on a rota basis. Between training we ate and slept, played football during the day and – age permitting – went to the pub in the evening. It was a great way to get back into the routine of training at the end of the summer holidays.

I soon made it a habit to enjoy the fun and stimulation of going away on training camps. During my time at university, we used to organise pre-season and mid-season camps in the New Forest and at Featherstone Castle in Northumberland. When I spent a year studying in Russia, I went away to a training camp in the Caucasus in the refreshingly named spa town of Mineral Waters. At the end of my first year of study in the States, I spent three weeks training in Vancouver on the west coast of Canada before returning to Britain to run in the 1988 Olympic Trials.

Training-camp life, as I was then experiencing it, centred on the enjoyment of being away with friends and travelling to new places. In my school and college days, running camp was about training and living together with other members of the club as we targeted our efforts towards a common goal. The places I travelled to in Russia and Canada enjoyed an ideal climate for distance running. I also appreciated the opportunity to learn from the other athletes and coaches with whom I was training. Our coach in Russia, for instance, was Nikolai Sviridov, who had placed fifth in the 1972 Olympic 10,000m. In Canada I trained with two Canadian Olympians, Peter Butler and Paul Williams. Already at this early stage, these aspects of training-camp life started to play a big motivating role in my running – and would continue to do so for many years to come.

ALTITUDE AND WARM WEATHER

When I moved to Marlborough in the summer of 1989, Bruce was keen for me to experiment with training at altitude. The use of altitude training as a means of boosting the oxygen-carrying capacity of distance-runners had been commonly practised around the time of the 1968 Olympic Games in Mexico City. But through the 1970s and 1980s, it had fallen out of fashion among the majority of the world's best runners. Bruce himself had taken part in some trials to test the benefits of altitude training during his own competitive career in the late 1960s, and had followed this with two years in Kenya in the early 1970s where he had worked as a coach to some of Kenya's top runners. Now, in the late 1980s, the Kenyans were beginning to emerge as the dominant force in the world of distance running. Besides, at that time the world-record holder at 10,000m, Arturo Barrios of Mexico, and at the marathon, Belayneh Dinsamo of Ethiopia, both lived and trained at altitude. It seemed to be a case of, 'If you want to beat them, join them.'

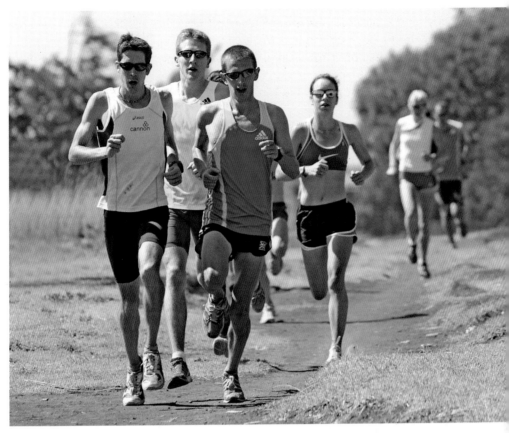

Lee Merrien, James Wilkinson, John Beattie and Steph Twell enjoy the Kenyan sunshine

In early December 1989 we were on a plane to Kenya, leaving behind us the cold of the British winter. It was a welcome change to be training in vest and shorts in the warm African sunshine, and such a boost to my winter's training. I caught the bug and never looked back. Over the following nine years I regularly went back to Kenya for training, nearly always over the Christmas period to escape the worst weather of the British winter.

For the first three or four years our training base was the Naro Moru River Lodge, on the western edge of Mount Kenya, at an altitude of 6400 feet. Together with Bruce and Sue and a group of training partners from home, we lived in self-catering cottages. We would train on the foot-slopes leading up the mountain as well as on the plains extending west to the Aberdare Hills. (Rarely would we get a chance to train with Kenyan runners, since at this time most of them trained either in army camps around Nairobi, or at their homes in the Eldoret region in the western part of the country.) We were surrounded by stunningly beautiful scenery. We enjoyed days of unbroken sunshine. We

Training with the Kenyans in 1992. Between 1986 and 1999 John Ngugi (in blue on far left) and Paul Tergat (in white on far right) each won five world cross country titles

also warmed to the friendliness of local people and the encouragement of interested onlookers, not to mention the spontaneous involvement of excited youngsters.

On one training stay in Kenya in February 1992, I spent three days at the Kenyan National Training Camp, which was being held at St Mark's Teacher Training College near Embu. As expected, the training regime was tough; yet, in the environment of other motivated athletes, I rose eagerly to the challenge. On several days we did three training runs. On the so-called 'rest day' – it included only *one* training session! – we got up shortly before six, were driven by bus 12 miles down the hillside, and then told to run back through the coffee plantations to the camp. On returning to the camp, I was told: 'Today we must rest, because tomorrow will be very hard.' So rest I did, as another day of 25 miles of running (including some tough hill climbs) lay ahead.

There was an overriding sense of doing the training together and helping each other get through the programme. I was frequently exhorted to eat more *ugali* (a common Kenyan dish made from maize-meal) 'because tomorrow we need to be very strong'. Here too, the group dynamic was central to the success of the training.

LIFE IN A TRAINING CENTRE

While Kenya fast became my favourite winter training location, during the European summer from 1991 onwards we regularly went to train at altitude in Font Romeu, a French National Training Centre in the eastern Pyrenees. The great advantage of Font Romeu lay in the fact that the centre is a purpose-built multi-sport complex. Athletes live and train on-site, with meals provided. Situated at an altitude of 6000 feet, the centre houses a tartan running track,

Q&A WHAT BENEFIT CAN I GET FROM
OXYGEN TENTS?

Few people have the luxury of going away from home for a number of
weeks to train at altitude. However, a 'home-based' alternative is now
available through the use of oxygen tents where an altitude environment
can be simulated in your own home. The idea is that you can increase
your haemoglobin concentration by sleeping in an oxygen tent without
any disruption to your normal training environment – you 'live high,
but train low'. As with real altitude training, best results are likely to
be achieved after first experimenting with different altitude simulations
and different durations of time spent sleeping in such conditions.

several gymnasia, swimming pools, Jacuzzi and sauna rooms, and good
medical facilities. It is surrounded by miles of scenic running trails. Typically in
the summer, the sun shines all day long; yet the cool, dry mountain air ensures
near-perfect running conditions.

During my stays in Font Romeu I usually trained harder than I did at home,
yet the training took place in an environment where all my other needs – in
the form of meals, rest and recuperation – were taken care of. I was also away
from the distractions of home and able to concentrate on the business of
training, and recovering from training. Besides the specific training benefits,
there was also the fun and stimulation of living in the presence of other
highly motivated athletes, with whom I trained and relaxed after the training
was done. As the years went by, I developed many friendships with other
international athletes whom I met at Font Romeu.

LEARNING FROM OTHERS

Looking back over training camps I have enjoyed in recent years, I can recall
many instances where I have benefited from sharing knowledge with other
athletes and coaches. I have picked up ideas on altitude training from José
Marin, a former athlete and now Spanish race-walking coach. I have observed
the training regime practised by a group of Mexican distance runners under
the supervision of the well-known marathon coach Rodolfo Gomez; and have
trained alongside Australia's marathon legend, Steve Moneghetti. I have
discussed ideas with many of Italy's top distance-running coaches, including
Luciano Gigliotti who coached the 1988 Olympic Marathon champion
Gelindo Bordin. I also learned some new methods of marathon training from
Dieter Hogan, former coach to the three-time Boston Marathon winner Uta

Pippig. In short, training camps have provided a great opportunity to learn from and share ideas with others.

Training camps offer more than shared experiences of training. They also give you an insight into the lifestyle of other runners and the approach they take to their sport. In this respect Dieter Baumann, the 1992 Olympic 5000m champion, was one of my role models for learning how to get the best out of yourself. On camps where we trained together, both in Kenya and in Europe, it became apparent how focused Dieter was on getting the most out of every training session. An easy recovery run was approached with the same seriousness as a hard workout: every session had a purpose in the overall plan. Dieter was a great performer – both on and off the track – when it came to the big occasion. No doubt this explains why his training, though a vital part of his preparation, always remained one step removed from what his sport was really about – namely, the cut and thrust of competition. These were qualities that I wanted to make my own. It was fun spending time with Dieter. And some of his motivation to succeed also rubbed off on me.

'I TRAIN, THEREFORE I AM'

Throughout my international career, I often gained a clearer sense of purpose about my training by going away to a training camp. When I stayed at home I could train well, but there were always other things that demanded my attention. When I was away at a training camp, my sole reason for being

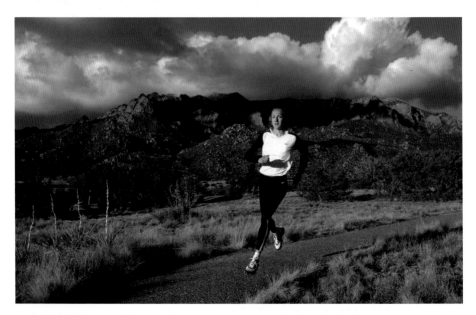

Paula Radcliffe, training here in Albuquerque, New Mexico, has been a great advocate of training at altitude in mountain sunshine

VIEW FROM THE ROAD
Jonathan Young: The benefits of running breaks

Jonathan Young enjoys a regular running holiday in Scotland
All my marathons have been memorable experiences but after my third one I was looking for a way of breaking out of my usual routine. A running holiday in Scotland proved to be the perfect answer. So one November I spent a weekend at Balmoral Castle with 'Running the Highlands'. Before going, I had a vision of endless runs over windswept moors but this holiday and three more I've done since then have been a great break and refreshment for me. On the holiday, over a long weekend, there are guided runs tailored to individual ability. But I have found the real benefit of the weekends to be the other running-related activities on offer which keep me motivated towards my running. I've heard talks by Olympians, expert coaches, nutritionists, exercise scientists and physiotherapists. I've run a VO_2 max test on a treadmill and discussed the results with a sports physiologist, allowing me to adapt my training to the results. I've learned new stretching and stability exercises that have helped prevent injury and I've even had massages to treat my tired limbs. The more intangible benefit of the weekends has been the buzz and stimulation from time spent with other runners of different abilities, but all with very positive outlooks and one main goal – to improve their running.

there was to train. To this end, I often scheduled periods away in training camps during the most important phase of a build-up to a major race. It invariably happened also that my increased focus on training while away in a camp fed my confidence as I prepared for competition.

Training camps are both good for your health and good for fitness. If you're lucky or resourceful enough to get a taste of training-camp life for yourself, I'm sure it will give your running a boost and only make you hanker for more.

KEY POINTS
• Enrich your running experience in a training-camp environment
• Consider ways in which you can enhance your running by imitating the routine of the full-time athlete.

USEFUL TIPS
Putting your running first

Have you ever wanted to get really serious about your running? Not to have to compromise your training at every turn because of other commitments in your life? Well, just maybe, running a marathon might be the time to break out of your normal, hectic stream of activities and indulge in a more running-centred approach to life. Whether you're running your marathon as a once-in-a-lifetime experience or having a second or third crack at it, your heightened focus on running need only last for the two to three months leading up to your marathon. I'm sure you won't regret it! Not all of you will be in a position to take up each of the suggestions that follow, but I hope there's at least something that might grab your fancy and become a reality for you in the midst of your otherwise busy lives. After all, where there's a will...

- *Be a full-time athlete for a day*. Arrange a workout with a group of running friends. Finish your session at a sports centre where you have time to stretch properly at the end of a hard session. Even better, jump in the pool for 10 minutes to relax those weary muscles. Refuel as you go with a bagel, banana and fruit juice. After a proper meal back home, have a lie-down to speed the process of recovery – for today, the shopping/ironing/cooking/cleaning can wait a while longer. Once in a while, arrange to have a massage or see a physiotherapist to check that you remain in good working order.
- *Be a full-time athlete for a weekend*. Your business associate has golfing weekends away, your best friend goes off to music festivals, and your kids have sleepovers – but you've never yet experienced a weekend given over exclusively to training. If you can't find them advertised in the running magazines, then create your own. All you need are a few training partners, a venue with plenty of good off-road running, and a comfortable place to relax over some good food.
- *Be a full-time athlete for a week*. The ideal option is a week away on a training camp with other runners in the Algarve or on Lanzarote (as regularly advertised in the monthly running magazines). Here you'll meet up with others who share your enthusiasm for training. You'll also be able to pick the brains of more experienced runners and coaches who are on hand to pass on advice. The low-cost, stay-at-home substitute involves using your week's holiday from work to enjoy more time to rest after your hard training sessions. Take advantage of your free time to have a massage or sauna. Make sure your training – including time for refreshment and relaxation – is finished before you attend to other matters.

TRAINING CAMP IN KENYA
NYAHURURU, DECEMBER 1998

My first exposure to Kenyan training camps was in 1992, when I attended the National Team camp prior to the 1992 World Cross-Country Championships. That was back in the days when Ngugi still reigned supreme on the country, William Sigei had yet to emerge as a future 10,000m world-record holder, and the softly spoken Paul Tergat had not yet competed outside Kenya (although in 1992 he had just won his first national title at the Kenyan Cross-Country Championships).

Over many winters since then, I have enjoyed training with Kenyan runners on their home soil in warm African sunshine. Though some of the names and faces of the emerging stars of Kenyan distance-running change from one year to the next, what seldom seems to change is the athletes' determination to make it to the top. If anything, their desire to succeed only seems to increase as the competition gets fiercer.

The Central Highlands of Kenya in early December enjoys a great climate for runners. As our training camp in Nyahururu (at 7800 feet and 150 miles north of Nairobi) is only two miles from the equator, a day in winter is the

Training with Kenyans in Nyahururu in 1998

same as in summer: the sun rises shortly after 6.00a.m. and sets shortly after 6.00 p.m. Midday temperatures peak at around 25°C.

It's December 1998 and I'm in the company of over 50 international-level runners from 800m to the marathon, who are disciplined and motivated to train hard. At the same time, they are welcoming to outsiders and sociable when it comes to relaxing in the sunshine after training. Our diet is simple yet nutritious: toast and jam for breakfast; beef or vegetable stew with rice for lunch; *ugali* and chicken for dinner. Snacks between meals come in the form of fruit or grilled corn-on-the-cob. Kenyan *chai* (drunk with hot milk and spoonfuls of sugar) always does a good job of refreshing weary athletes. The less appealing aspects of training-camp life start with the 5.45a.m. alarm for the first morning run at 6.00a.m. Though we enjoy 12 hours of unbroken sunshine each day, it's still dark as we start our run in tracksuits, and sometimes even hats and gloves. Our next problem crops up when we're back from our run and discover that there's no water in the hotel. This means having to wash ourselves down from a tub of cold water, clean our teeth from bottled water and leave the washing of our dirty shorts and socks until the supply has returned. Then it's down for tea and toast in the restaurant. This brightens us up for a while, but we're still a little tired when the second morning run comes around at 10.00a.m.

Kenyan athletes have the knack of helping each other get through a day's training. It's what I call 'the *sukumawiki* effect': *sukumawiki* literally means 'push the week forwards' and happens to be the Swahili name for a favourite athletes' meal of spinach stew. For every complaint of tiredness comes in equal measure an encouragement to keep up and stay the course.

Once we reach lunchtime the day's training is over, and we have all afternoon and evening to recover. The Kenyan secret to being able to train hard is simply to allow yourself time to rest hard after the training.

Our regular routine is a 6.00a.m. run (of between 40 and 60 minutes), followed by a second morning session at 10.00a.m. (sometimes a hill workout, or a track session, or some sprint drills on the sports field). Sometimes we just do one (slightly longer) early morning run and get into resting mode straight after our 8a.m. breakfast.

By midday it's getting quite hot, and we amble up into town to a local restaurant for a hot lunch of *ugali* and beef stew. Then it's back to the hotel for a long afternoon rest. As dusk approaches, we start to think ahead to our next workout as word spreads around the camp about the following morning's training...

One Thursday morning this involved a 50-minute early morning run, followed at 10a.m. by a 4km time trial. This was the start of a long selection process that culminates each year in late February when the Kenyan teams for the World Cross-Country Championships are finally decided. On this occasion I finished a minute behind former world cross-country silver medallist Paul Koech, yet Paul himself only managed third behind James Koskei, one of Kenya's emerging young talents.

On the same day, 50 miles to the east in Nanyuki, where the Kenyan Air Force has a base, a 12km time trial was won by Benjamin Limo (who went on to win the 1999 World Cross-Country 4km title). Ismail Kirui placed sixth and Joseph Keter, the 1996 Olympic 3000m steeplechase champion, 10th. A fortnight earlier in Nairobi, at the Kahawa Barracks Trials, the winner had been Simon Maino, the 1998 Commonwealth 10,000m champion.

If I ever needed one, here was another reminder of the wealth of talent in Kenyan distance-running. While what seem like swarms of Kenyan distance-runners racing on the track and cross-country each year in Europe, there are even greater swarms still back in Kenya competing to get on the next plane out of Nairobi.

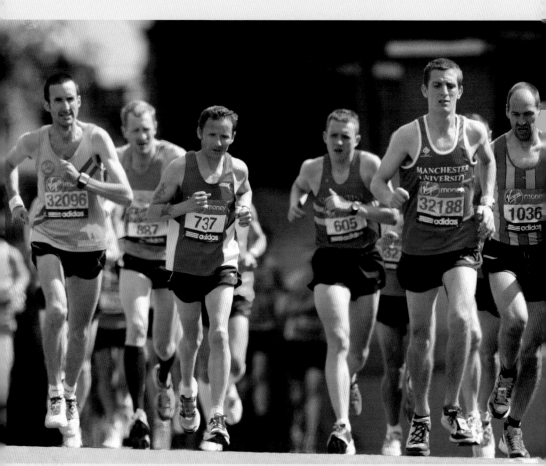

2012 London Marathon participants push on along the Embankment in the final stages of the race

PICKING UP THE PIECES

In the introduction to this book I asked what it took to run a marathon. The most basic requirement, I suggested, was a commitment of effort and determination to get you through the training and around the 26-mile distance. If you're prepared to make that commitment, then you should consider yourself capable of completing a marathon – regardless of athletic talent or proven running ability.

A BRIEF SUMMARY

My advice in the early chapters of this book was based on this premise. Apply yourself seriously to your training and make a wholehearted effort to get the most out of your running, and you will be rewarded with a fulfilling marathon experience. Sound planning (Chapter 2), followed by methodical, race-specific training (Chapter 3) sustained by a good diet and sufficient recovery periods (Chapters 4 and 5), should form the basis of your preparation. Couple this with a determination to avoid illness and injury, and the right mental approach to competition (Chapters 6 and 7), and you should have every chance of completing your marathon successfully.

If you are a regular runner, you will have higher ambitions for your marathon. You will be interested not just in completing your event, but also in running a *good* one. In other words, you will be hoping to achieve a particular time goal for the race. The second half of this book is written with these higher goals in mind. You may want to take a more serious approach to planning out your training for the whole year (Chapter 8). Considering ways of improving your racing strategy (Chapter 9) and making running more of a priority in your life (Chapter 10) may also contribute to better performances in your running.

At whatever level you aspire to compete, one thing should have become clear

Less than three months after her disappointment at the 2004 Athens Olympics, Paula Radcliffe bounced back in style by winning the first of her three New York City Marathon titles

in the course of reading this book: *the marathon is a tough event*. Even assuming that your training and race experiences turn out well, your powers of endurance will be stretched to the limit as you learn to cope with high levels of fatigue and discomfort. But, as I pointed out in the book's introduction, the marathon presents other equally demanding hazards: compared to other distance races, there are so many more things that can go wrong in the marathon.

In this last short section, I want to consider where some of these problems might arise. Some are potentially avoidable, given careful planning and preparation. Others are simply beyond human control – and then it is how you respond to the problem that marks you out as a winner or a loser.

AVOIDABLE PROBLEMS

From earlier chapters in this book you will have noted where mistakes can arise in your marathon preparation. The first and most obvious is that you are not ready to run the distance simply because you have not done enough or the right kind of training. Even if you've done the right training, you may pay the price for not paying sufficient attention to your diet or to the importance of refuelling and rehydrating during and after training and in the course of your marathon. The use of poor or inappropriate footwear and running gear might cause you a problem. If you don't give enough thought to your race day travel arrangements, you might find yourself arriving late for the start of the race. You may simply be found out on race day because, even though you're at a peak of physical fitness, you fail to approach the event with sufficient caution and respect for running at a level pace. Another common problem can come from a change of routine in the final few days before the race. Sometimes this may be as basic as getting sick from eating a new food the night before the race, or falling ill from travelling or from a change in climate as you travel to the race venue. Look back to some of the earlier chapters if you are still unclear about how to avoid these all too common mistakes.

Sometimes it's only by making mistakes that you more fully understand the importance of getting things right. So, if you have a disappointing race performance, be prepared to learn from your experience and make amends next time. Analyse what went wrong (e.g. were you unable to peak at the right time? Or was your pace judgement at fault? Or did you not devote sufficient attention to your mental preparation?) and take action. Often it helps to discuss these matters with a coach, or if necessary, a sports psychologist.

UNPREDICTABLE PROBLEMS

Despite all your best efforts, you may find that you succumb to illness or injury in the days leading up to the race. Even the world's best marathon runners are not immune to such misfortune: there are countless examples where last-minute problems have put paid to all the hard months of training that have gone before. Even in the race itself the unexpected sometimes happens, as Haile Gebrselassie experienced within the space of a few minutes in London in 2007. Feeling relaxed and still full of running for the first 17 miles of the race, he suddenly suffered severe breathing problems caused by his asthmatic condition, which forced him to step off the road a few minutes later. Other misfortune may also be just around the next corner: Abdelkader El Mouaziz, a previous race winner in London, was tripped and fell badly at the halfway point in the 2002 London Marathon, yet still managed to finish in fourth place. The list of potential hazards waiting to ensnare you – from a twisted ankle to a dog bite, from food poisoning to the common cold – is enough to make you feel at least a little 'on edge' as you approach the day of your marathon.

How should you react if you are unlucky enough to confront such adversity? Sometimes, the illness or injury leaves you with no other option than to withdraw from the race. You should then ensure that you have fully recovered before committing yourself to another race. If you're in any doubt about the state of your recovery, give yourself time to do at least one good training session before deciding on your next race.

Often, it is harder to decide whether or not you should pull out from your intended marathon. You appear to be over the worst of your injury or illness, but you have not had time to test yourself in training as you have eased down for competition. Withdrawing from the race would represent a huge disappointment. Not only would you be missing the race that for so long has been the focus of your training; you might also feel that you were letting down all your friends who are supporting you for charity. On the other hand, by starting the race you would run the risk of performing well below your expectations – or even of not finishing – with little room for a second chance. With the marathon, caution should be your guide. In the long run, you may be doing more harm to your health and your confidence by taking risks. If in doubt, seek counsel from a coach or friend who, while understanding your motivation, can offer a more dispassionate opinion.

Remember too that if you do decide to withdraw from a marathon, there are plenty of other races keen to have your entry. Unlike the London Marathon, many of these can be entered on the day.

Whichever way you decide, your race performance will in part be determined by how well you can put misfortune behind you. In other words, focus on what you can still achieve – even if you have to revise your goals – rather than on what you might have achieved had things turned out differently. On the eve of the 1996 Olympic Marathon in Atlanta, Britain's best female runner of the 1990s, Liz McColgan, suffered an insect bite on her foot. With the next Olympic opportunity four years away, she had little option other than to start the race in Atlanta: her 16th place finish, while a personal disappointment, demonstrated her fortitude in overcoming adversity.

Your ability to deal with the unexpected – for instance, a last-minute change in the weather, in the route of the marathon or in race-day arrangements – will depend on your state of mental preparation. You should make contingency plans where you can foresee possible problems. You should also rehearse that feeling of staying calm and unperturbed by these external events. Your performance is the one thing over which you can have the most influence, so it is vital that you stay focused on this task as the race approaches.

MOVING ON

What happens once your marathon has been run?

Your first priority should be to restore your life to a semblance of normality. Having let your training and thoughts about running your marathon occupy many of your waking moments over the past few weeks, you (and no doubt other members of your family) will benefit from switching off from running for a while and devoting more time to those things that were neglected during your marathon preparation.

When the highs and lows of race day have worn off, you will be in a better frame of mind to consider the 'Never again!' you uttered as you crossed the finish line at the end of your marathon. It would *not* be unnatural, having done all that training, for you soon to rediscover the urge to lace up your running shoes once more...

There is something about running that draws us back for more. Whatever our age or experience, running provides us with new challenges. Despite the saying, 'you're only as good as your last race,' many runners are more interested in their *next* one. I hope that the same is true for you.

KEY POINTS
- Learn from your mistakes
- Resist the temptation to run your marathon if you are still suffering the effects of illness or injury
- Be prepared to revise your goals if your plans change, and focus on what is ahead
- Give yourself a good recovery period after your marathon.

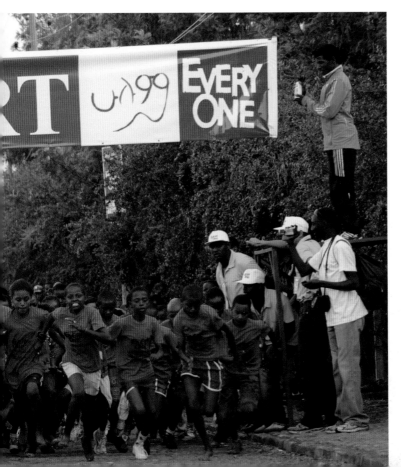

Haile Gebrselassie (top right) starts the children's races at the annual Hawassa races outside his resort hotel in southern Ethiopia

197

LEARNING FROM MY MISTAKES
ATHENS, AUGUST 1997

Shortly after running the 1997 London Marathon, I had to decide whether or not to accept my place to run for Britain in the 1997 World Championship Marathon in Athens. I wanted to compete for Britain in another championship race, but I was unsure whether I was ready to put myself through another three months of gruelling marathon training so soon after my last period of marathon preparation.

In the end I decided to accept my place to run in Athens. I am always motivated to train hard for championship races. There was the added attraction of running over the ancient course from Marathon to Athens. I also felt that I might not need to train quite as hard or for quite as long as I had for the London race – since I already had a good bank of fitness from earlier in the year.

BUILD-UP
Three weeks after the London Marathon I was back into training and planning my build-up for the race in Athens. Within a week of starting some hard sessions, I began to experience discomfort in my foot – similar to when I was injured in 1995, only now the problem was in my other foot. Once again, I was reduced to doing much of my training in the pool and on the exercise bike.

As the pain abated, I went back to see the specialist who had advised me about my previous foot injury, and was relieved to be told that the problem had eased sufficiently for me to resume normal training. There were now 7½ weeks remaining until the marathon – just enough time, I felt, for me to return to peak fitness. Ahead of me was a three-week stint back at Font Romeu, where I hoped to complete the hardest phase of training before the marathon in Athens.

GOING FOR BROKE
Over those next three weeks I trained harder than ever before. Assisted by Keith Anderson, who on the eve of his 40th birthday proved to be one of my most enthusiastic training partners, I made the mistake of trying to extend the limits of my training. Once we were over our initial five-day period of acclimatisation, we followed a five-day cycle of training that included a long run of 35–40km, a tempo run of 20–25km, and a 10km workout – plus two days in which we sometimes went beyond our stated intention of running at a steady pace. Over the course of the next 15 days we completed this cycle three times, which meant running 10 hard workouts in the space of just over two weeks. Over the entire 21-day period of our stay, we ran over 400 miles.

We were relieved to get to the end of our stay at altitude still in one piece. We had survived without succumbing to injury or illness, and without breaking down with exhaustion – or so we thought.

On my return home I had an easy week of training, reducing the volume from around 140 miles per week to just over 100. With two weeks to go, I did my last really hard session before the race. I still felt tired while doing this session, but I knew there were a further two weeks of tapering before the day of the marathon.

A FLAT BATTERY

With 12 days to go, I went out to a training camp in Italy, to acclimatise to the Mediterranean heat that we would have to endure in Athens. I continued to reduce my training, in the hope that I would soon start to get some bounce back into my legs as the race drew nearer.

What I actually experienced, however, was quite the opposite. Even going out for a short run felt like really hard work. My body seemed to be slowly grinding to a halt. I was still eating and sleeping normally, and wasn't feeling ill. It was just that I couldn't run. Whenever I tried to put one foot in front of the other and break out into a jog, I couldn't keep going for more than a few hundred metres – as if my body were failing to respond to its usual operating signals. Painfully, I was being made to realise that I would have to withdraw from the marathon in Athens.

LEARNING THE LESSONS

> '**I had learned the simple truth that more is not always better.**'

I had made the mistake of trying to play 'catch-up' with my original training schedule, which had been interrupted by another foot injury. My frustration at this setback had increased my determination to regain peak fitness, as a consequence of which I had taken too big a risk while training at altitude. I had crammed in too many hard sessions and not given myself sufficient recovery periods – especially important at altitude, where you need longer to recover after intense workouts. At the start of my preparation for Athens, I had acknowledged that I would not need to repeat the intensity of training that I had achieved for my two previous marathons. But I had strayed from these good intentions and, as a result, overdone my training.

I had learned the simple truth that more is not always better. I had trained harder than ever before in the run-up to the 1996 Olympic Marathon, and it had paid off. The same had again been true of my preparation for the London Marathon the following April. But now, in the build-up to Athens, I had overstepped the thin line between being super-fit and being over-trained. Now the training had to stop.

A last-minute offer to help out with the BBC commentary on the marathon in Athens distracted my attention from the obvious disappointment of not being able to take part in the race myself. On my return home, I had a number of blood tests to see if my problem could be more clearly identified, and thereafter took my customary end-of-season break. My recovery period would be longer than usual, however, to give myself every chance of making a full recovery from what I had suffered over the summer. Then it was back to the drawing board – time to plan my next campaign.

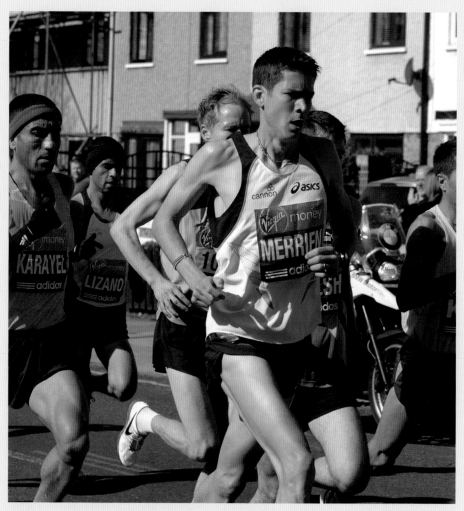

Hard work pays off: Lee Merrien started out as an 800m runner (PB 1:49:97), but finally won selection for Britain's 2012 Olympic marathon team after running a 2:13:41 PB in London

APPENDICES

APPENDIX 1
Richard Nerurkar: career details

Date	Event	Finishing position	Time
	Championship marathons		
31 October 1993	World Cup Marathon	1st	2:10:03
14 August 1994	European Championship Marathon	4th	2:11:56
12 August 1995	World Championship Marathon	7th	2:15:47
4 August 1996	Olympic Marathon	5th	2:13:39
22 August 1998	European Championship Marathon	8th	2:14:02
	City marathons		
23 May 1993	Hamburg Marathon	1st	2:10:57
19 March 1995	Kyongju Marathon	2nd	2:11:03
13 April 1997	London Marathon	5th	2:08:36
	Track championships		
27 August 1990	European Championship 10,000m	5th	28:07
26 August 1991	World Championship 10,000m	5th	27:57
3 August 1992	Olympic 10,000m	17th	28:48
	Cross-country championships		
19 March 1989	World Cross-country Championships	49th	n/a
24 March 1990	World Cross-country Championships	18th	n/a
24 March 1991	World Cross-country Championships	52nd	n/a
21 March 1992	World Cross-country Championships	15th	n/a
11 December 1994	European Cross-country Championships	25th	n/a
	Best times: track		
15 July 1992	3000m – IAAF Nice Grand Prix	9th	7:48:00
10 August 1990	5000m – IAAF Brussels Grand Prix	5th	13:23:31
10 July 1993	10,000m – IAAF Oslo Grand Prix	4th	27:40:03
	Best times: road		
31 July 1994	10km – BUPA Great Welsh Run	2nd	28:25
17 October 1993	10 miles – Twickenham Cabbage Patch	1st	46:02
14 April 1996	Half-marathon – Paris Humarathon	4th	1:01:06

APPENDIX 2
Training for the half-marathon

The table below should help you plan out your own half-marathon training programme according to your level of fitness and time goals. The ideal length of time for your build up is 12 weeks, comprising 10 weeks of good training followed by a two-week taper. You should aim to run at least one race (e.g. 10km or 10 miles) midway through your build-up.

Level	Time goal (hours)	Sessions per week	Miles per week	Weekly long run* (miles)	Quality sessions**
Beginner***	1:50–2:20	4–5	15–25	5–8 (10)	Fartlek + tempo run
Regular runner	1:30–1:50	5–6	30–40	8–11 (13)	Repetitions + tempo runs
Advanced	Faster than 1:30	6–7	40–50	12–14 (15)	Repetitions + 1:30 tempo runs

    *   On a regular basis (longest)
   **   In addition to easy/steady running and long run
  *** This follows on from the programme for beginners in Chapter 1

Over the course of your build-up you should aim to increase the volume of some of your quality sessions. A beginner, for example, might start with a total of 10–12 minutes of fast running (2 × 5 min or 3 × 4 min) and aim to build up to 20+ minutes (3 × 7 min or 4 × 6 min). The key sessions for the half-marathon, in addition to your long run, are the repetition workouts where you are running for an interval of 4–10 minutes at close to your 10km racing speed. You can vary your sessions of faster running by changing the length of interval. For a change from interval running, you might decide to do some hills, a pyramid session (e.g. 2 sets of 1 min–2 min–3 min–2 min–1 min) or some fartlek.

A sample week's training halfway through the build-up might look something like this:

Day	Beginner	Regular	Advanced
Monday	30 min easy	35 min easy	35 min easy
Tuesday	35 min inc. 5 × 1 min + 5 × 30 secs fast	6 × 3 min fast, 2 min recovery	6 × 1km, 2 min recovery
Wednesday	Rest	30 min easy	45 min easy
Thursday	3 × 5 min fast, 2 min recovery	10 min + 5 min + 5 min fast, 3 min recovery	6–7 miles fartlek
Friday	Rest	Rest	Rest
Saturday	35 min easy	30 min easy	3 × 2 miles, 3 min recovery
Sunday	7 miles long run	10 miles long run	13 miles long run
Total	22–24 miles	34–36 miles	45–47 miles

Your two-week taper for the half-marathon should follow a similar pattern to your marathon training: training volume is reduced and sessions of faster running are designed to get you used to running at your intended race pace.

APPENDIX 3
Marathon training programmes

(a) For sub-5:00 marathon
(b) For sub-4:00 marathon (i)
(c) For sub-4:00 marathon (ii)
(d) For sub-3:30 marathon
(e) For sub-2:45 marathon
(f) For sub-2:20 marathon

Key
s = seconds
km = kilometres; hr = hour(s)
m = metres; 2 min = with 2 minutes recovery
mins = minutes; * = @ marathon pace

Note: All weekly totals are given in miles.

(a) Programme for sub-5:00 marathon

Week	Monday	Tuesday	Wednesday	Thursday	Friday	Saturday	Sunday	Total
1	Rest	20–25 mins easy	Rest	6 × 1 min fast, 2 min	Rest	30 mins steady	1:30hrs walk/jog	18
2	Rest	6 × 200m hills	20–25 mins easy	2 ×(1km fast, 4 mins walk)	Rest	35 mins steady	1:30hrs walk/jog	22
3	Rest	6 × 2 mins fast, 2 mins jog/walk	20–25 mins easy	40 mins steady	Rest	25 mins fartlek	1:45hrs	25
4	Rest	8 × 1 min fast, 2 min	4 miles easy	Timed run over 3 miles	Rest	4 miles steady	1:45hrs	28
5	Rest	3 × 1km, 4 min	3 miles easy	3 miles easy + strides	Rest	Rest	10km race	18
6	Rest	4 miles easy	4 miles easy	8 × 150m hills	Rest	5 miles steady	2hrs	28
7	Rest	6 × 3 mins fast, 2 min	3 miles easy	Timed run over 5 miles	Rest	10 × 1 min/ 1 min fartlek	2:20hrs	30
8	Rest	3 × 8 mins, 3 min	4 miles easy	8 ×(90s, 90s)	Rest	4 miles easy or rest	Half-marathon race or 2:40hrs	35
9	Rest	3 miles easy	5 miles easy	10 + 6 + 3 mins fast, 3 min	Rest	4 miles easy	3hrs	35
10	Rest	4 × 1km, 3 min	Rest	Timed run over 6 miles	Rest	4 miles easy	1:30hrs	25
11	Rest	3 × 10 mins*, 3 min	Rest	4 miles easy + strides	Rest	10 × 1 min/ 1 min fartlek	10km race	20
12	Rest	2 × 1 miles*, 3 min	Rest	20 mins easy	Rest	15 mins easy or rest	Marathon	10 + race

*For sessions of faster running, run 1 mile (8–10 min) easy warm-up/warm-down

(b) Programme for sub-4:00 marathon (i)

Week	Monday	Tuesday	Wednesday	Thursday	Friday	Saturday	Sunday	Total
1	Rest	40 mins easy	Rest	6 × 1 min fast, 2 min	Rest	30 mins steady	1:30hrs walk/jog	18
2	Rest	10 × 1 min, 2 min	4 miles easy	2 × (1km fast, 4 mins walk)	Rest	35 mins steady	1:30hrs walk/jog	22
3	Rest	8 × 5m hills	4 miles easy	40 mins steady	Rest	25 mins fartlek	1:45hrs	25
4	Rest	8 × 2 mins, 2 min	5 miles easy	Timed run over 3 miles	Rest	4 miles steady	1:45hrs	28
5	Rest	4 × 1km, 3 min	4 miles easy	3 miles easy + strides	Rest	Rest	10km race	18
6	Rest	6 miles easy	5 miles easy	8 × 150m hills	Rest	5 miles steady	2hrs	28
7	Rest	15 + 10 + 5 mins fast, 3 min	4 miles easy	Timed run over 5 miles	Rest	10 × 1 min/ 1 min fartlek	2:20hrs	30
8	Rest	3 × 8 mins, 3 min	4 miles easy	8 × (90s, 90s)	Rest	4 miles easy or rest	Half-marathon race or 2:40hrs	35
9	Rest	5 miles easy	8 × 1 min, 1 min + 8 × 30s, 30s	10 + 6 + 3 mins fast, 3 min	Rest	4 miles easy	3hrs	35
10	Rest	4 miles easy	5 miles steady	Timed run over 6 miles	Rest	4 miles easy	1:30hrs	25
11	Rest	3 × 10 mins*, 3 min	5 miles easy	4 miles easy + strides	Rest	10 × 1 min/ 1 min fartlek	10km race	20
12	Rest	2 × 1 mile*, 3 min	Rest	20 mins easy	Rest	15 mins easy or rest	Marathon	10 + race

*For sessions of faster running, run 10–12 min warm-up/warm-down

(c) Programme for sub-4:00 marathon (ii)

This programme is designed for those who have time only for three running-training sessions each week. The Tuesday–Thursday–Sunday routine can be adapted to individual need – the main thing is to space a non-running day after each running day. While the easy running sessions from other schedules are replaced here by non-running days, there is also slightly more emphasis on making more effort in the longer runs and in the sessions of faster running. Because of the reduced number of running days, you should also try to have longer warming-up/cooling-down periods for the sessions of faster running.

Week	Tuesday	Thursday	Sunday	Total
1	5 × 2 mins, 2 mins + 5 × 1 min, 1 min	6 miles steady	1:15hrs	22
2	4 × 1km, 3 min	8 miles steady	1:30hrs	24
3	10 × 200m hill	15 mins + 10 mins + 5 mins, 4 min	2hrs	27
4	Timed run over 6 miles	9 miles steady	2hrs	31
5	10 × 200m hill	8 miles steady	10 mile race	28
6	8 miles steady	6 × 1km, 3 min	2:30hrs	31
7	8 × 2 mins, 2 min	11 miles steady	2:45hrs	35
8	15 mins + 15 mins + 10 mins, 4 min	5 miles steady	Half-marathon race	31
9	8 miles steady	6 × 1km, 3 min	3hrs	35
10	6 miles steady	Timed run over 6 miles	1:45hrs	27
11	15 mins + 10 mins + 5 mins, 3 min	6 × 2 mins, 2 min	1hr	21
12	2 × 1 mile*, 3 min	3 miles easy	Marathon	8 + race

*For sessions of faster running, run 15–20 min warm-up/warm-down

(d) Programme for sub-3:30 marathon

Week	Monday	Tuesday	Wednesday	Thursday	Friday	Saturday	Sunday	Total
1	5 miles easy	5 × 3 mins, 2 min	5 miles easy	5–6 miles fartlek	Rest	6 miles steady	12 miles	40
2	5 miles easy	10 × 45s hills	5 miles easy	Timed run over 4 miles	Rest	6 miles steady	14 miles	45
3	5 miles easy	2 × (2km + 1km), 3 min	5 miles easy	5–6 miles fartlek	Rest	8 × 1 min hills	16 miles	50
4	Rest	8 × 2 mins, 2 min	5 miles easy	5 miles easy + strides	Rest	3 miles easy	10km / 10 mile race	30
5	Rest	6 miles easy	a.m. 4 miles easy p.m. 12 × 1 min, 1 min	5 miles easy	1 × 2 miles, 4 min + 2 × 1 mile, 3 min	6 miles steady	16 miles	50
6	5 miles easy	a.m. 4 miles easy p.m. 5 × 1 km	5 miles easy	a.m. 4 miles easy p.m. 5–6 miles fartlek	Rest	Timed run over 5 miles	18 miles	55
7	5 miles easy	a.m. 4 miles easy p.m. 10 × 2 mins, 2 min	5 miles easy	3 × 2km, 3 min	Rest	8 miles steady	20 miles	55

8	5 miles easy	a.m. 3 miles easy p.m. 3 × 1 mile, 3 min	6 miles easy	5 miles easy + strides	Rest or 4 miles easy	Rest	Half marathon race	40–45
9	Rest	6 miles easy	a.m. 5 miles easy p.m. 6 × 1km, 3 min	5 miles easy	a.m. 5 miles easy p.m. 6 miles brisk	4 miles easy	22 miles	60
10	Rest	5 miles easy	a.m. 3 miles easy p.m. 6 miles steady	3 × 10 mins, 3 min	5 miles easy	10 × 400m, 90s	14 miles	45
11	4 miles easy	6 miles brisk	5 miles easy	6 miles steady + strides	Rest	3km + 2km + 1 km*, 3 min	8 miles	35
12	3 miles easy	2 × 1 mile*, 2 min	Rest	3 miles easy	Rest	2 miles easy or rest	Marathon	15 + race

(e) Programme for sub-2:45 marathon

Week	Monday	Tuesday	Wednesday	Thursday	Friday	Saturday	Sunday	Total
1	a.m. 5 miles easy / p.m. 5 miles steady	6 × 3 mins, 2 min	a.m. 5 miles easy / p.m. 5 miles steady	5 miles fartlek	4 miles easy or rest	5 miles steady	14 miles	50
2	a.m. 5 miles easy / p.m. 5 miles steady	8 × 150m hills	a.m. 5 miles easy / p.m. 5 miles steady	Tempo run over 5 miles	5 miles easy	5 miles steady	16 miles	55
3	a.m. 5 miles easy / p.m. 5 miles steady	4 × 1 mile, 2 min	a.m. 5 miles easy / p.m. 5 miles steady	6 × 250m hills	5 miles easy	2 miles easy + strides	10km/ 10 mile race	50
4	a.m. 5 miles easy / p.m. 5 miles steady	10 × 2 mins, 2 min	a.m. 5 miles easy / p.m. 5 miles steady	3 × 2km, 3 min	a.m. 5 miles easy / p.m. 5 miles steady	5 miles steady	18 miles	60
5	a.m. 5 miles easy / p.m. 5 miles steady	8 × 150m hills	a.m. 5 miles easy / p.m. 5 miles steady	6 miles easy + strides	Rest	2–3 miles easy	10–20 mile race	50–60
6	5 miles easy	6 miles fartlek	a.m. 5 miles easy / p.m. 5 miles steady	8 × 1km, 3 min	a.m. 5 miles easy / p.m. 5 miles steady	Timed run over 8 miles	20 miles	65

Week								Total
7	a.m. 5 miles easy p.m. 5 miles steady	1-2-3-4-3-2-1 min pyramid	a.m. 5 miles easy p.m. 5 miles steady	4 × 2km, 3 min	a.m. 5 miles easy p.m. 5 miles steady	5 miles steady	22 miles	70+
8	a.m. 5 miles easy p.m. 5 miles steady	2 × 1 mile, 2 min + 2 × ½ mile, 90s + 4 × 400m, 1 min	5 miles easy	5 miles easy + strides	Rest	2–3 miles easy	Half marathon race	45
9	5 miles easy	6 miles steady or easy fartlek	a.m. 5 miles easy p.m. 5 miles steady	3 × 3km, 3 min	a.m. 5 miles easy p.m. 5 miles steady	8 × 2 mins, 2 min	24 miles	75
10	5 miles easy	a.m. 4 miles easy p.m. 7 miles brisk	5 miles easy + strides	2 × 5km*, 4 min	5 miles easy	6 miles steady	15 miles	55
11	6 miles easy	6 miles fartlek	5 miles easy	8 miles brisk	Rest	5 miles steady + strides	10 miles	40
12	5 miles easy	2 × 1 mile*, 2 min	Rest	3 miles easy + strides	Rest	2 miles easy or rest	Marathon	15+ race

(f) Programme for sub-2:20 marathon

Week	Monday	Tuesday	Wednesday	Thursday	Friday	Saturday	Sunday	Total
1	a.m 6 miles easy; p.m. 6 miles steady	a.m. 4 miles easy; p.m. 4 × 1 mile, 2 min	12 miles easy	a.m. 6 miles easy; p.m. 8 miles steady	6 miles easy	8 miles inc. 20 mins fartlek	16 miles	80
2	a.m 6 miles easy; p.m. 6 miles steady	a.m. 4 miles easy; p.m. 3 × 3km, 3 min	12 miles easy	a.m. 6 miles easy; p.m. 8 miles steady + strides	a.m. 4 miles easy; p.m. 6 × 800m, 2 mins	Rest	18 miles	80
3	a.m 6 miles easy; p.m. 6 miles steady	a.m. 5 miles easy; p.m. 8 × 1km, 90s	13 miles easy	a.m. 5 miles easy; p.m. 6–7 miles fartlek	8 miles steady	40 mins tempo run	18–20 miles	90
4	a.m 6 miles easy; p.m. 6 miles steady	a.m. 5 miles easy; p.m. 4 × (1600m + 400m), 1 min/2 min	13 miles easy	a.m. 5 miles easy; p.m. 5 miles easy + strides	Rest	4 miles easy	10km race	65
5	a.m 6 miles easy; p.m. 6 miles steady	16 miles easy	a.m 6 miles easy; p.m. 10 miles steady	a.m. 5 miles easy; p.m. 4 × 2km at marathon pace, 1km at 30s slower	Rest	a.m. 8 miles inc. 20 × 30s, 30s; p.m. 4 miles easy	20 miles	90
6	a.m 6 miles easy; p.m. 10 miles steady	a.m. 6 miles easy; p.m. 6 × 1 mile, 2 min	14 miles easy	a.m. 5 miles easy; p.m. 8 miles easy + strides	a.m. 5 miles easy; p.m. 5 miles steady	4 miles easy	Half-marathon race	90

7	Rest	5 miles easy	8 miles easy	a.m. 5 miles easy p.m. 5 miles easy	10 miles steady	8 miles inc. 20 mins fartlek	22–24 miles	70
8	a.m 6 miles easy p.m. 6 miles steady	5 × 2km at marathon pace, 1km 30s slower	14 miles easy	a.m. 6 miles easy p.m. 6 miles steady	a.m. 5 miles easy p.m. 10 × 2 mins, 90s	10 miles easy	24 miles	95
9	a.m 6 miles easy p.m. 6 miles steady	a.m. 6 miles easy p.m. 2 × 2 miles, 2 mins + 2 × 1 mile, 90s	14 miles easy	a.m. 6 miles easy p.m. 10 miles steady	a.m. 5 miles easy p.m. 5 miles steady	8 miles inc. 20 × 30s, 30s	20 mile tempo run	100
10	Rest	a.m. 5 miles easy p.m. 6 miles steady	10 miles easy	10 miles easy	a.m. 5 miles easy p.m. 6 miles steady	a.m. 2 × (8 × 400m, 45s), 3 mins; p.m. 5 miles easy	14 miles	75
11	Rest	a.m. 4 miles easy p.m. 2 × 6km at marathon pace, 4 mins	a.m. 5 miles easy p.m. 5 miles steady	6 miles easy	a.m. 7 miles inc. 20 × 30s, 30s; p.m. 5 miles easy	Rest	12 miles	55
12	5 miles easy	8–10 miles steady finishing briskly	Rest	4 miles easy + strides	Rest	2–3 miles easy	Marathon	20 + race

APPENDIX 4
Weights and circuits for marathon runners

As with the stretches on pp. 5–9, it is beyond the scope of this book to provide anything more than general guidelines on weights and circuits. For more specific information and illustrations of the exercises, refer to an established book, like Anita Bean's *Complete Guide to Strength Training* (A & C Black).

How much and how often? In general, the more time and energy you devote to your running training, the less you can give to alternative forms of training. This means that the best time to do this form of training is during a period of relatively little running. Three short (20-minute) sessions per week is better than a once-weekly hour-long session; do half this amount for 'maintenance' during a period of harder running training.

Main objectives: all-round body conditioning, addressing in particular any muscle weaknesses and thus reducing the likelihood of injury.

Weights or circuits? Do what you enjoy most and what comes more easily – circuits, for instance, though more enjoyable when done with a group in the gym, can be done in your living room at the end of a run. The key thing is to focus on your own weaknesses in core muscles (*see* tables below).

GENERAL GUIDELINES FOR USING WEIGHTS

- Use weight machines, rather than free weights, to isolate key muscle groups.
- Seek advice from a gym instructor about operation of machines.
- To guard against overstrain, do more repetitions with lighter weights.
- Aim to maintain a smooth, steady rhythm as you lift – don't jerk your effort.

ADDRESSING WEAKNESSES USING WEIGHTS

PART OF BODY	PURPOSE	EXERCISE
Quadriceps, gluteals and hamstrings	To maintain strength balance between quadriceps and hamstrings, and protect against overstrain	Leg presses; hamstring curls; quadriceps lifts; squats with bar on shoulder
Back	To improve running posture and prevent weaknesses leading to hip and hamstring problems	Lateral pull-downs; back extensions
Abdominals	To maintain efficient running posture and stabilise trunk	Sit-ups, perhaps even with bean-bag weight on top of stomach
Arms	To maintain good form, especially at end of race	Triceps dips

ADDRESSING WEAKNESSES THROUGH CIRCUIT TRAINING

For a 20-minute session, complete the programme below twice, i.e. 2 × 10 min circuit (8 × 60 seconds, with 15 seconds recovery).

PART OF BODY	PURPOSE	EXERCISE
Back	Arches	Lie on front with arms in 'hands-up' position; keeping lower body on the floor, raise upper body (from waist up) off floor
Abdominals	Crunches	Lie on back with knees pulled up towards stomach, feet held together off floor and hands behind head; raise head so that elbows touch knees
Hips and gluteals	Side leg raise*	Lie on side, resting only on elbow and side of bottom foot (and knee if necessary). Raise top leg for 10 sec hold, and repeat 4 times
Arms and chest	Press-ups	Do not let back arch by keeping head, neck and spine in straight line
Back and abdominals	Straight leg raise*	Press-up position, but resting on forearms (not hands); keeping back straight and squeezing buttocks together, raise alternate legs off ground for 30 sec hold
Abdominals	Scissors	Lie on back with legs raised slightly off floor – one bent, the other extended – with one arm extended forwards towards knee, the other back behind head; alternately move forwards and back opposite arm and leg
Hips and hamstrings	Straight leg extension*	Lie on back with knees bent and feet on floor. Raise hips off ground, keeping weight on head, shoulders and arms, hips held high and buttocks squeezed. Alternately extend one leg towards ceiling for 30 sec hold
Arms	Running arms	Standing with one foot forwards, shoulders relaxed and elbow fixed at 90°, adopt fast running-arm action

*In contrast to the other exercises involving fast continuous motion, these exercises strengthen the muscle groups through a process of holding in a stable position.

In recent years world champions Mo Farah and Paula Radcliffe, have led the way for British distance running

INDEX

ALSO AVAILABLE FROM BLOOMSBURY

ISBN 978-1-4081-3324-8

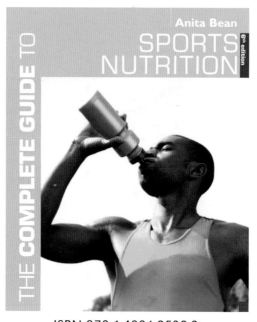

ISBN 978-1-4081-0538-2